Graham,

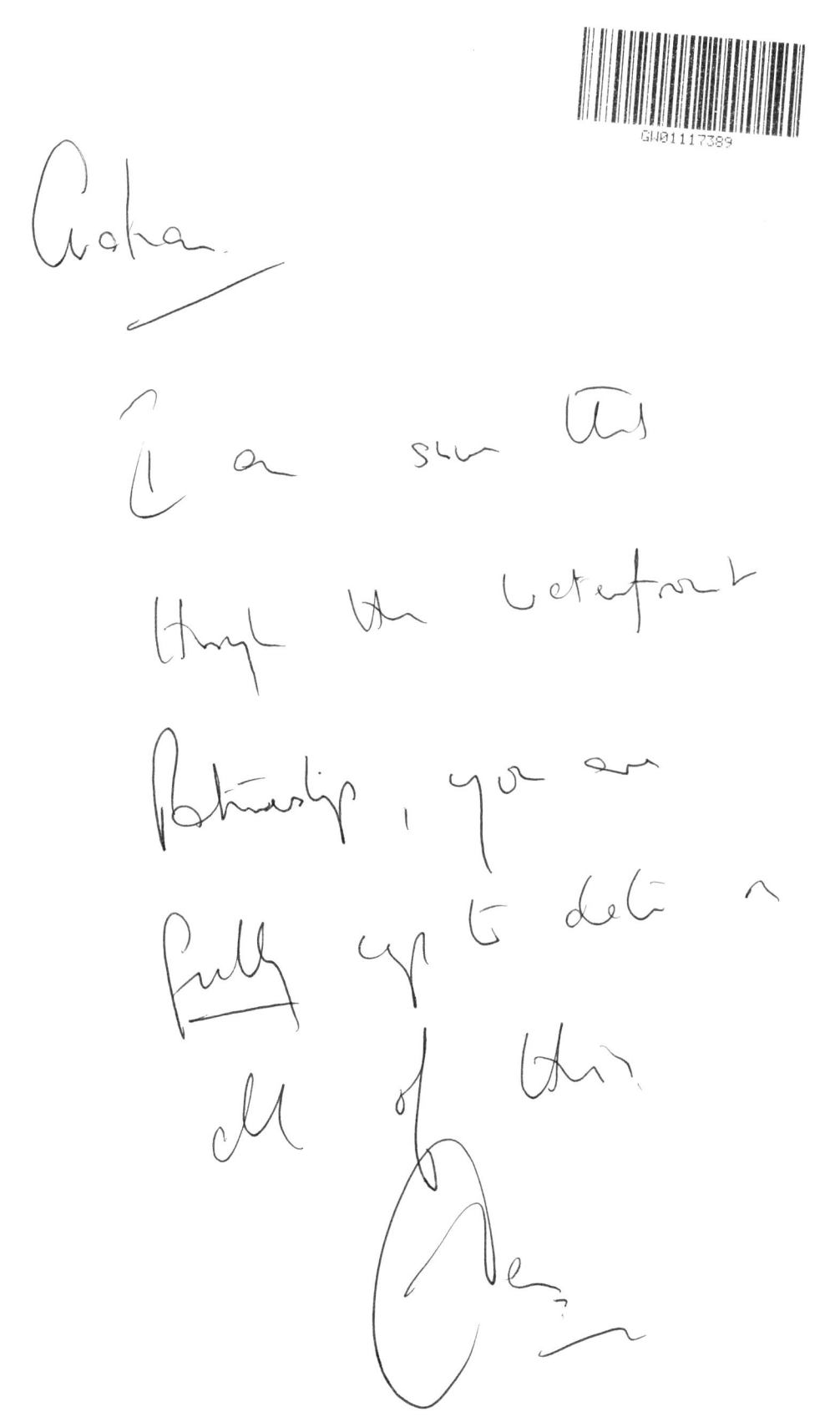

I am sure that through the Waterfront Partnership, you are fully up to date on all of this.

[signature]

SHIPPING
FUTURES

SHIPPING FUTURES

BY
JAMES GRAY

SECOND EDITION

|L|L|P|

LONDON   NEW YORK   HAMBURG   HONG KONG
LLOYD'S OF LONDON PRESS LTD.
1990

Lloyd's of London Press Ltd.
Legal Publishing and Conferences Division
One Singer Street, London EC2A 4LQ
Great Britain

USA AND CANADA
Lloyd's of London Press Inc.
Suite 308, 611 Broadway,
New York, NY 10012, USA

GERMANY
Lloyd's of London Press GmbH
59 Ehrenbergstrasse, 2000 Hamburg 50
Germany

SOUTH-EAST ASIA
Lloyd's of London Press (Far East) Ltd.
Room 1101, Hollywood Centre
233 Hollywood Road
Hong Kong

First published in 1987 as *Futures and Options for Shipping*

Second edition 1990

© James Gray, 1987, 1990

British Library Cataloguing in Publication Data

Gray, James Whiteside
 Shipping futures.–2nd ed.
 1. Freight transport services: Shipping services. Futures markets
 I. Title II. Gray, James Whiteside. *Futures and options for shipping*
 332.644

ISBN 1-85044-322-X

All rights reserved. No part of this publication may be reproduced, stored in a retrieval system, or transmitted, in any form or by any means, electronic, mechanical, photocopying, recording or otherwise, without the prior written permission of Lloyd's of London Press Ltd

Text set 11 on 13 pt Sabon by
Megaron, Cardiff, Wales
Printed in Great Britain by
Bookcraft Ltd., Midsomer Norton

FOREWORD

The use of freight futures is still relatively new to the shipping world, having been introduced as recently as May 1985. It is remarkable that an industry which experiences greater volatility in its basic commodity—freight rates—than perhaps any other has taken so long to develop a concept which has formed part of the everyday strategy of traders in metals, oils and agricultural products for many years.

The Baltic Exchange, one of the original sponsors of the Baltic International Freight Futures Exchange, continues to provide the daily Index upon which the futures contracts are based, and to support the development of the market.

This book, which updates and expands upon previous publications by the same author, is therefore most welcome and will play an important part in the continuing process of education. Hedging, which will undoubtedly play an increasing role in the strategy of shipowners, charterers and operators worldwide, is still insufficiently understood by many in our industry—an omission which will be rectified by close study of the chapters which follow.

PAUL VOGT
Chairman,
The Baltic Exchange

PREFACE

When Michael Grey of Fairplay (now of *Lloyd's List*) asked me to write *Financial Risk Management in the Shipping Industry* in 1986, I little guessed that I would enter a revised and expanded version under the title *Futures and Options for Shipping* for the BIMCO/Lloyd's of London Press Maritime Book prize in 1987. My only excuse for offering a third edition under the title *Shipping Futures* is that the concept of freight futures has moved on by a long way in the last three or four years, and that this book covers a fair bit of ground not covered in the previous two. To anyone who has been kind enough to buy all three books: Thank you, and I hope that you will not find this one excessively repetitive.

This, therefore, is a good opportunity to offer thanks to a number of people who have helped me hugely, not only in the production of this book but also in the work we have all done in the promotion of futures for the shipping industry over the last five years. GNI Ltd have been generous in allowing me the time and facilities for a variety of extra-curricular activities—the Commodities Division team as a whole are hard working, enthusiastic and very tolerant. The various boards, committees and secretariats with which I have had dealings have grown used to ignoring the worst excesses of my hyperbole and have been most helpful in producing this book. This particularly applies to Patrick Neave of BIFFEX. Hugh Morshead, Marketing Manager of GNI Ltd, and Sally Clubley, formerly energy desk manager at E D & F Man, author of *Trading in Oil Futures*, and now a consultant in the oil industry, have kindly provided chapters on subjects beyond my expertise.

I am indebted to Paul Vogt, Chairman of the Baltic Exchange, for a most kind foreword. Carol Springett has uncomplainingly produced a perfect typescript from a hieroglyphic and is in every respect indispensable.

And last my family, Sarah, John and Olivia, consistently continue to put up with me not being there, or spending too much time at my desk when I am.

It is perhaps worth saying that I have used some chapters in this book as a platform for some of my more outspoken or individualistic views about shipping and about futures. These views are entirely my own, and these people bear no kind of responsibility. Nor, of course, do GNI Ltd nor any of the exchanges and committees which are mentioned.

London, July 1990   JAMES GRAY

CONTENTS

Foreword by Paul Vogt, Chairman, The Baltic Exchange   v
Preface   vii
List of Illustrations and Figures   xii

1 A FUTURE FOR SHIPPING: STOPPING THE RISK PENDULUM   1

2 PHYSICAL OR FUTURES HEDGING?   13

1. Physical hedging   14
2. Futures hedging: the principle   16
3. Futures hedging: how it works   18
4. How a futures market functions   21
5. The psychology of futures hedging   21

3 DRY CARGO FREIGHT FUTURES: THE BALTIC FREIGHT INDEX   25

1. The concept of cash settlement   25
2. How the Baltic Freight Index is constructed   27
3. How the BFI moves   30

4 HEDGING ON BIFFEX: THE PRINCIPLE   36

1. Freight futures hedging: the basic principle   36
2. Freight futures hedging: the simple stratagem   38
3. Freight futures hedging: some developments and refinements of the simple hedging stratagem   42

CONTENTS

5 HEDGING ON BIFFEX: THE DETAIL — 44
The calculation of the dry cargo freight futures hedge: — 44
  (1) The contract — 44
  (2) Correlation with the BFI — 48
  (3) Calculating the level of the hedge: voyage charters — 52
  (4) Calculating the size of the hedge: voyage charters — 57
  (5) Calculating the level of the hedge: time charters — 58
  (6) Calculating the size of the hedge: time charters — 60
Dry Cargo hedging using BIFFEX — 63

6 TANKER FREIGHT FUTURES: THE 1986 EXPERIMENT — 65

7 TANKER FREIGHT FUTURES: THE 1990 CONTRACT — 71

8 OIL FUTURES FOR THE SHIPOWNER
by Sally Clubley — 79

Basis trading — 81
Sale on buyer's call/trigger pricing — 83
Exchange for physicals — 84
Over-the-counter markets — 86

9 THE SHIPOWNER'S USE OF FINANCIAL FUTURES AND OPTIONS *by Hugh Morshead* — 89

1. Financial hedging using futures — 90
2. Financial hedging using options — 92
3. Conclusion — 95

10 THE PRACTICALITIES OF FUTURES TRADING — 97

1. The relationship with the futures broker — 99
2. How to trade on a futures market — 109
3. What does it cost? — 113

11 MAKING MONEY WITH FUTURES — 119

The aim of the speculator — 120

CONTENTS xi

12 THE FUTURE FOR FUTURES 129
1. The eighties 129
2. The nineties 132
3. The twenty-first century, or sooner? 137

13 SHIPPING MARKET RISK: TOWARDS A NEW ERA 141

APPENDIX I: FURTHER READING 147

APPENDIX II: THE BALTIC FREIGHT INDEX 149

A How the BFI is computed 149
B Daily route indices 150
C Quick calculation of index expectations 152

APPENDIX III: THE BFI CONSTITUENT ROUTES: CURRENT AND HISTORICAL 153

APPENDIX IV: BFI: DAILY LEVELS SINCE 4/1/85 159

APPENDIX V: TABLE OF BIFFEX CONTRACT AVAILABILITY 169

APPENDIX VI: EXTRACT OF ENERGY FUTURES CONTRACT 171

APPENDIX VII: EXTRACT OF FINANCIAL FUTURES CONTRACT 173

APPENDIX VIII: GLOSSARY OF STANDARD TERMS 175

Index 177

LIST OF ILLUSTRATIONS AND FIGURES

Figure 1 BFI, 1985/90   3
Figure 2 The risk/reward parabola   10
Figure 3 BFI 1985/90 — linear   29
Figure 4 BFI 1985/90 — year-on-year comparison   32
Figure 5 Charterer's decision-making process   39
Figure 6 Shipowner's decision-making process   40
Figure 7 Comparative chart of BIFFEX prices   46
Figure 8 Example of reasonable correlation. BFI vs trade route   49
Figure 9 Example of reasonable correlation. BFI vs Basket of trade routes   50
Figure 10 Futures prices and Gulf/Japan equivalents   57
Figure 11 Baltic Tanker Index 1984–1985   68
Figure 12 Baltic Tanker Index 1986   68
Figure 13 Tanker spot rate trends   72
Figure 14 Oil output and tanker demand   73
Figure 15 Bank of England US dollar trade-weighted index   89
Figure 16 US Federal funds rates, 1980/90   90
Figure 17 Graph of DM 62 call option at expiry   93
Figure 18 Graph of the 92.50 put option at expiry   93
Figure 19 Completed trading form   107
Figure 20 The clearing house system   114
Figure 21 Technical analysis examples   122

CHAPTER 1

A FUTURE FOR SHIPPING: STOPPING THE RISK PENDULUM

"There can be no denying that the current crisis in the shipping industry is one of the most severe in its turbulent history. The industry will no doubt emerge from it leaner, hungrier and probably altogether better than it was, but what is to prevent another equally catastrophic crisis occurring again at the end of another 20-year cycle? Then 20 years after that, and so on? Analysis of the shipping market (at least since the Second World War) indicates a regularly recurring lemming-like tendency on the part of many of the major players. Every time demand (in the form of cargoes needing to be shipped) exceeds supply (in the form of ships trading), even if that imbalance is known to be temporary, there is a rush of new-building orders, a sharp increase in second-hand prices, a curiously short-sighted but overwhelming desire on the part of banks to lend money for maritime enterprises, and sooner or later the inevitable collapse. The catastrophe seems to occur at the peak of optimism, when the shipyards' orderbooks are overflowing, the lay-up berths empty and the scrapyards almost out of business. Such an analysis of the post-war shipping industry indicates a haphazard, confused, almost random, attitude to the trends and swings and cycles which occur in all industries. We seem as an industry consistently to get the long-term pattern wrong, and both bull and bear markets nearly always take us completely by surprise."

This prophetic paragraph formed the opening of chapter 1 of the first edition of this book. It was written at the low point of the dry cargo market slump in 1986/1987, when the Baltic Freight Index touched its all-time low of 553.5 (on 31 July 1986), when the time charter rate for a panamax bulkcarrier for a transatlantic round-voyage was around $2,250, when the per metric tonne rate for grain loading in the US Gulf, discharging Japan was $7.65 and when you could buy a reasonable secondhand panamax for $5.5 million.

At that time, most players and observers in the shipping industry were verging on the suicidal. Shipowners, brokers, charterers, managers, ship financiers, marine underwriters, P & I clubs, ship chandlers, builders, analysts, journalists and pundits alike seemed agreed that the dry cargo market as we had known it was finished. Some said that the ownership and management of the fleet would swing inexorably to the heavily subsidised and labour-rich Pacific Basin. Others argued that the days of the independent shipowner tramping his vessels on the spot market were over, and that shipowning would increasingly become a function of central government. Bankruptcies, distressed sales, lay-up, scrapping, redundancies, cutbacks, gloom, doom and disaster were the order of the day. We had come to the edge of the world, and any day now might well topple over it.

But within days—in early September 1986—there was a sudden increase in interest in the grain market, some of the ships which had been anchored "off Key West, waiting for orders" suddenly disappeared from brokers' tonnage lists, the offices of the Soviet chartering agent Sovfracht got busier, rates ticked up a little, those charterers who had been waiting in the wings in the belief that there was "no great rush to fix a ship in this market" stepped into the market place to take tonnage, and that remarkably accurate and sensitive indicator of the dry cargo market the Baltic Freight Index (BFI) turned round and started its inexorable move upwards. And from that time until May 1989, with the exception of expected seasonal dips, it never really looked back. (As the chart, figure 1, indicates.)

And at the time of writing (in early 1990), things are looking pretty rosy both for the tanker and the dry cargo market. The age profile of the tanker fleet, coupled with buoyant demand for oil and increasing environmental concerns about tanker safety, leads most observers to expect an increasing demand for a decreasing fleet, with the concomitant of firm rates for tankers for some years to come. (This theme is developed in chapter four.) A strong tanker market means that combination carriers (which for the sake of the uninitiated are able to carry either oil or dry cargo) will be trading in oil. And since combination carriers are one of the largest swing factors on the supply side of the dry cargo supply/demand equation, this is in itself good news for the dry cargo market. On the bulkcarrier side, too, things are looking pretty healthy. A booming world economy has resulted in good demand for coal and ore. And a series of demographic and weather factors has maintained demand from the grain and sugar markets. On the supply side of the

HIGH 1751.00 16/5/89   LOW 554.00 5/8/86   LAST 1215.00

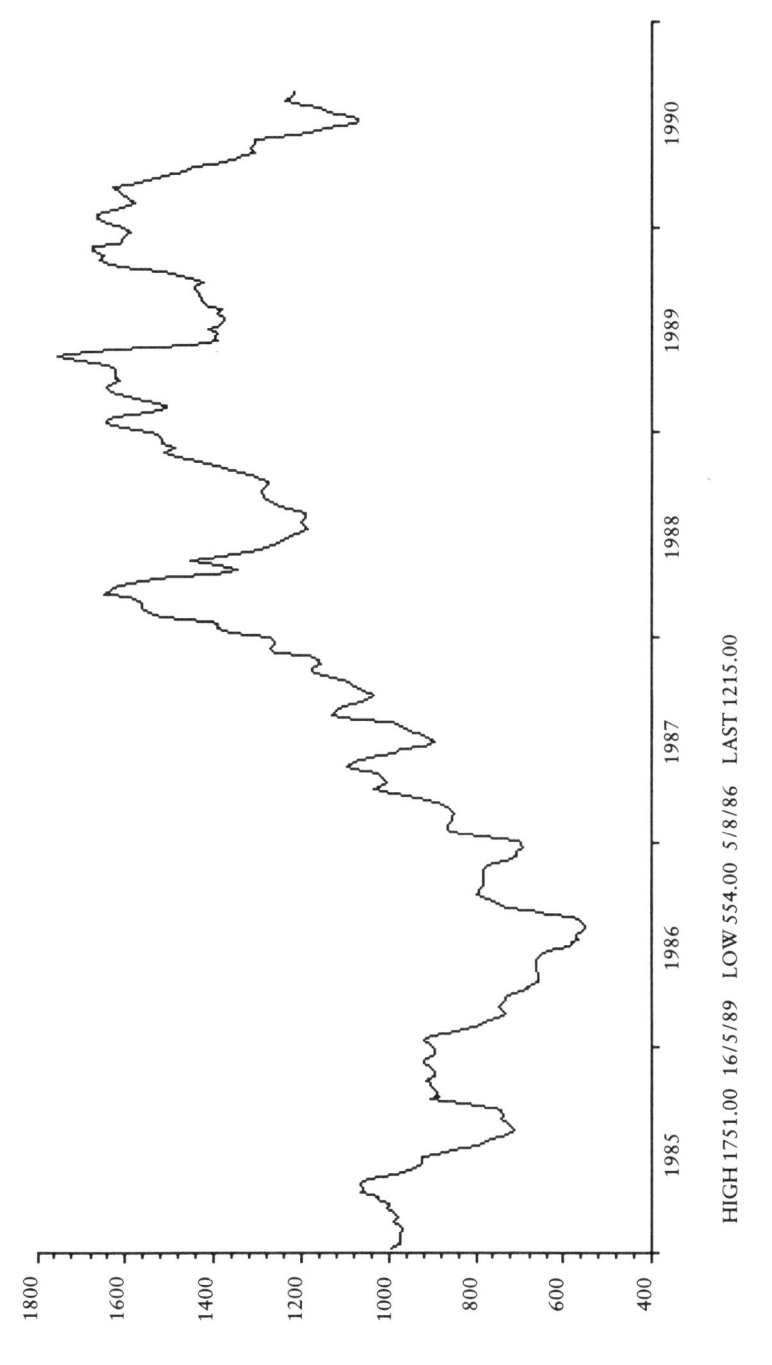

Figure 1. Baltic Freight Index, 1985/90

equation, such a massive quantity of tonnage was scrapped in the mid/late 'eighties that the current world fleet is virtually fully utilised, and is—by and large—trading profitably.

A panamax bulkcarrier trading in the Atlantic at present is probably averaging a return of $14,000 a day. That yardstick of the dry-cargo market, Gulf/Japan panamax-sized grain, is trading at roughly $28; capesizes (130,000 deadweight tonnes and above) are probably achieving something like $3.60 per deadweight tonne per month. Everything is looking pretty rosy in the garden, and looks like staying that way (or getting better) for some time to come. Or does it?

Analysis of the supply/demand equation in the bulkcarrier market shows that the supply side actually looks set to rise substantially within the next twelve months. According to Fairplay (Newbuildings, 25 January 1990) there is a current total world orderbook of nearly 52 million deadweight tons and 1,400 vessels, 32% of that being bulk carriers (225 vessels, 110 of which are "handysized", 60 panamaxes and 55 capesizes). And most of that tonnage is due to be delivered in the second half of 1990 and first half of 1991. The existing fleet is fully utilised, with a minimum of lay-up, scrapping, slow-steaming or other inefficiency. Effectively all vessels ever likely to trade are now trading, and with freight rates and second-hand prices as high as they are neither scrapping nor lay-up seem likely to increase in volume, at least in the short term. So the overall supply of dry-cargo carrying capacity seems set to rise steeply over the next twelve months or so. Perhaps not quite so rosy, then, but still not too bad.

How do things look on the demand side of the equation? Unfortunately not all that bright either. Few economists seem to doubt that the OECD nations may face at best zero growth, perhaps recession within the next year or two. The implications for the steel industry, and therefore for those mainstays of the bulkcarrier market, coal and iron ore, are obvious. A straw in the wind for a forthcoming recession in the steel-making industry, despite a continuing (although perhaps temporary) growth in Japanese steel production, may be a surprising collapse in the steel price. The collapse in the Tokyo Stock Exchange in the early part of 1990 may turn out to have been a leading indicator for the freight market.

And the outlook on the grain side of the demand equation is probably not too optimistic either. It is certainly true that a fundamental strand of Perestroika must be that Gorbachev feeds, and is seen to feed, his people. Certainly, while his hard currency lasts, he will be buying US and South American grain (as he did in the last quarter of 1989). But for how long? The Soviet economy seems to be completely ruined. Grain purchases can only be financed by sales of gold and oil, but both of those are delicate markets which could easily be upset by excessive Soviet selling. And the whole of Eastern Europe and Soviet Russia are now starting to look so politically and economically unstable that a large concerted grain purchasing programme such as that in previous years is probably unlikely for some years to come.

So the supply side of the equation is rising, the demand side is, or soon will be, falling. The logic seems inescapable: that we can expect a fall—and probably a severe one—in at least the panamax market during the second half of 1990/first half of 1991.

Surely not, I hear you say. Surely all the pundits can't be wrong. Current rates, albeit stronger than they were, still do not justify the strength in the secondhand market. And newbuilding prices are worse. The market must strengthen further. Otherwise how will all the current newbuilding orders pay for themselves? How indeed!

As I said in the first paragraph of the first chapter of the first edition of this book (writing, let it be remembered, at the low point of the market in 1986): "The catastrophe seems to occur at the peak of optimism, when the shipyards' orderbooks are overflowing, the lay-up berths empty and the scrapyards almost out of business." Indeed so.

The freight market, in common with many other markets, seems to turn at the moments of greatest pessimism and of greatest optimism. This phenomenon is convincingly explained in a fascinating and seminal examination of mass psychology and the cyclical behaviour of the shipping market by Michael Hampton, an economist with Chase Manhattan Bank, in *Long and Short Shipping Cycles* (Cambridge Academy of Transport, 1989).

In very simple terms, he tries to prove the existence of discernible very long-term cycles in the shipping market, first spotted in the world economy by the analyst Kondratieff. The turning points in these long-term cycles, Hampton argues, are characterised by the deepest gloom and pessimism at the bottom end and the greatest optimism for the future at the top end.

As soon as people start talking about a "new era" or the market now being "on a plateau from which it can take off", or when you hear people say that freight rates only now justify second-hand and newbuilding prices, you can be almost certain that we are heading for a crash. When banks are once again increasing the percentage of the value of a ship they are prepared to lend (which they are at the time of writing), when second-hand prices become hugely inflated, when new speculative money is being invested in ships (not only by banks, but perhaps more worryingly by private investors, either for tax reasons, as in the Norwegian K/S schemes, or dazzled by hot-shot Wall Street salesmen, as in the public flotation of shipping ventures in the States), when governments (and Quangos such as the General Council of British Shipping) start talking of governmental subsidy either for shipping companies or worse shipbuilding companies, when in so many other ways the shipping industry is as buoyant and optimistic as it is now, then it seems to me that we are very likely to be on the brink of a collapse to come.

This may be thought by some to be an idiosyncratic view. And I would be the first to admit that I am at best an armchair economist and that a thousand different events or influences may well interpose themselves, perhaps even between the time of writing and the time of publication of this book, to prove this gloomy prognostication wildly inaccurate. I will be only too happy if it is indeed wrong. A futures broker, I always argue, should have a clear and firm view of which way the market is going. Like anyone else, he will of course be wrong a great deal (although one hopes less than 50% of the time), but by clearly expressing his outspoken views of the market he is at least giving his clients an opportunity for discussion. Thesis and Antithesis produce Synthesis. So I stand a very good chance of being completely wrong in this prediction of a fall to come in the near future in the dry cargo market. But where I can be 100% certain, is in saying that the dry cargo market will collapse one day. When that will be, how far it will have risen in the meanwhile, how far it will fall, is a matter for judgement and opinion. But the inexorable truth is that one day—as it always has—the dry cargo freight market will assuredly collapse.

So what are we doing about it? Chapter 1 of the first edition of this book went on to ask:

What are we going to do in the future to try to prevent the same catastrophe again? Once the irresistible forces of capitalism have corrected the current imbalance in supply and demand, what economic, commercial or logistical structural changes must we make to protect our no doubt leaner and healthier industry from the same self-indulgent blow-out in the future?

And the book concluded:

The necessity to restructure the industry on a sound commercial basis is apparent to all. It is the view of the author that increased usage of futures hedging should be at least one main element in that restructuring. If the industry as a whole fails to grasp the opportunity offered, we will publish the second edition of this book during the next shipping collapse in approximately twenty years' time.

The purpose of this second edition, only four years after the first, and thankfully in advance of a shipping collapse to come, is to examine the extent to which the industry has restructured itself to control freight market risk, in particular to examine the shipping industry's usage of the futures markets as risk-control mechanisms, and perhaps to suggest how use of these sophisticated financial instruments may yet help to prevent, or to alleviate the harshness of, the collapse which the author, for one, believes that we are facing.

The problem facing the shipping industry could perhaps be over-simplified into one word: "Risk". How so? Of all the capitalist markets, the shipping industry is the least regulated, the most volatile, the least homogeneous and most diverse. Shipowners are spread all over the world geographically. They vary from the captain/owner of a 500 tonne coaster to the chief executive of a multinational shipping conglomerate, having control (albeit indirectly) over a fleet of perhaps as many as 500 ships. And within only a few sometimes loosely-enforced international conventions, these owners can buy and sell, man and victual, repair, maintain and trade their ships exactly as they like. Unlike, for example, the road haulage or air passenger industries which are so hide-bound by rules and regulations, permits and licences, and above all by restrictive practices (such as the control by IATA of the routes which the various airlines can ply), that it must sometimes seem almost impossible to earn an honest living, the shipping industry as a whole is virtually unfettered by national or international restraints.

This freedom, it must quickly be said, is demonstrably a "good thing". The right to do what you like, when you like with your money is one of the most basic rights of the Western World. It can on occasion, however, produce volatility of a scale and severity rarely seen in a more regulated, controlled or balanced business.

The disparate nature of the players in the shipping industry, and the lack of any kind of centralised control over supply and demand, means that under the right circumstances (and often for all the wrong reasons) all of the major players tend to do the same thing at the same time. So when a shortage of ships is forecast, the universal tendency is a rush to build them, producing a huge swing to an oversupply in the market. Chronic oversupply of tonnage leads to universal scrapping and a recovery in the market such as that experienced in 1986/90. In other words the freedom of action traditionally enjoyed by the shipping industry tends to produce exceptional volatility in the market. Freedom of action plus volatility equals, in capitalist terms, risk-unfettered and uncontrolled risk of the worst kind.

"However we do it", I said in the first edition, "the shipping industry will one day return to profitability when the supply/demand pendulum swings back the other way. What we should now be doing as an industry is studying ways of stopping the pendulum approximately at equilibrium, and then holding it there, without interfering with the individual rights and liberties of the shipowner". So the Holy Grail we should all be searching for while the market is in its current reasonable state is a way to stop the market pendulum. Risk and the resulting volatility are the root causes of its wilder swinging, so risk control of one kind or another is what is needed to steady it. If the shipowner can remove many of the financial risks of his business we will be well on the way to creating a balanced, reliable means of transport for the merchant or importer at a reasonable cost, together with a sensible profit for the shipowner. This utopia can and must be achieved if we are to avoid a return to the sort of slump we saw in the mid-1980s. The key to its achievement is a much more careful and scientific investment policy for the industry, which by definition will take account of, and limit and control, the risks which have always been inherent in the shipping business.

What, then, is the nature of these risks and what can we do to limit them? Let us first of all define business risk. Taking a risk in general terms, of course, is following a course of action the outcome of which is unclear. So the risk we are dealing with here is the purely financial risk of an investment failing to make a profit for the investor, or worse making a substantial loss for him. It is the risk of taking a commercial course of action in the shipping industry, the outcome of which (in terms of profit or loss) is unclear.

Risk of this kind is a fundamental necessity of all capitalism. Accepting a risk in return for a profit is indeed the most basic principle of capitalism. The shipowner accepts a risk which others are unwilling or unable to accept—all of the myriad risks inherent in buying, manning, running and maintaining a ship, loading a cargo, transporting it across thousands of miles of ocean, and finally delivering it to the receiver. All of these risks are unacceptable to the merchant, to the raw material producer and to the end-user. Taking such risks is the shipowner's business and they are risks which he cannot avoid. In return for accepting these risks the shipowner can expect to make a reasonable profit. So the first conclusion must be that risk equals profit under capitalism.

Secondly, it is often said that the size of the risk and that of the profit are likely to increase (and decrease) more or less in direct proportion to one another. The larger the risk involved in a particular enterprise, it is said, the larger the fee which can be charged, and therefore the larger the profit; and the smaller the risk, the smaller the profit. "Speculate to accumulate" is the old maxim, and it is applied as often to the shipping industry as to any other.

But is it true? We are speaking here of probabilities. At a certain stage, the risk of a venture increases to such an extent that it becomes increasingly unlikely that the venture will be successfully undertaken. Mathematically, therefore, we should think of "risk" and "reward" as a sort of equation. At risk = 0, reward is likely to be 0. As risk increases, reward increases perhaps as far as 50% risk. But as risk increases above 50%, reward will once again decrease, until, when risk is 100% (i.e., there is no chance of success), reward will again be at 0. So in broad terms the risk/reward equation can be thought of in terms of a parabolic graph along lines shown in figure 2.

In other words some risk is desirable since it itself generates profit. But profit must be maximised by limiting that very risk. The shipowner must on the one hand take physical and commercial risks to make his profit, while simultaneously on the other hand limiting that risk to within commercially manageable boundaries.

At first sight this might appear to be teaching my granny to suck

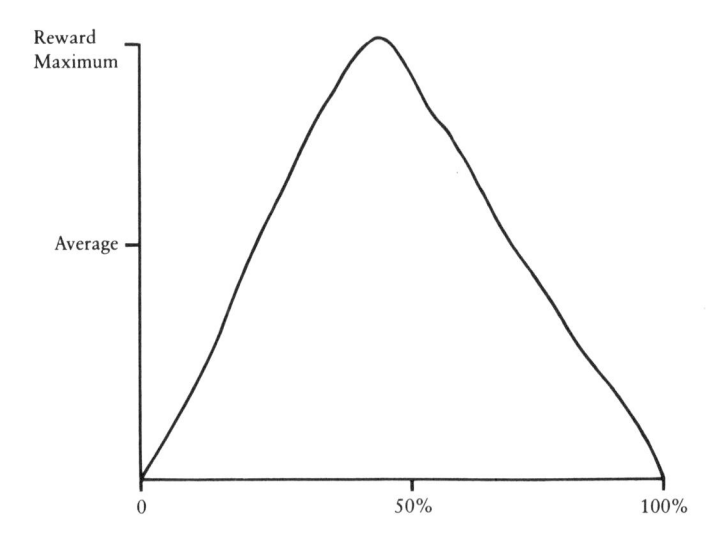

Figure 2. The risk/reward parabola

eggs! Of course, any businessman worth his salt knows that the larger the risk, the greater the return, until the risk is so large that you don't stand much chance of a return at all. Not only any businessman, but most gamblers, and certainly all bookmakers, know that. And the traditional shipowner sometimes looks like a cross between a businessman and a professional gambler. If he buys a secondhand vessel for $10 million, of course he assesses (or guesses) the likelihood of the market rising, the duration of the strong market, the life expectancy of the vessel, and its residual value as scrap. Of course he assesses all these things. And so does his lending bank. Or do they?

In reality do not most shipowners and their banks suffer from a Jekyll and Hyde type of schizophrenia—are their characters not often split between scientific industrialist and wild, gut-feeling gambler? How often over the last five years since the foundation of BIFFEX have I heard arguments from shipowners that the freight futures market is not for them. Their attitude is perhaps epitomized by one who is an active futures trader, but who never, but never, "goes short" of the futures market. He is always "long"—in other words always predicting a rising market, despite the fact that he is already gambling on a rising market by the very act of owning ships. "Mr Gray, if I thought that the freight market was going down, I would sell my ships and then I would not be a shipowner any more." Some shipowners seem to become so fixated by "talking the market up" that they become unable to foresee even the slightest possibility of a fall to come. Or others say "How can the market fall, when current rates, albeit better than they have been for years, are nowhere near good enough to justify current secondhand prices?"—ignoring the fact that the secondhand market is itself a hugely speculative bubble.

Yet another who visited me last year told the following tale: "In mid-1987 I had a million dollars in cash. My bank gave me another million, and I bought a bulkcarrier, which I have just sold for $9 million, netting me $7 million profit on $1 million investment, in the space of two years. That, Mr Gray, is why I am a shipowner. I'm not much interested in maintaining revenue flows. I make my money out of asset-plays." I am sure you do, and good luck to you. But what about the poor fool who is last in the asset chain? The bankrupts of 1986 might have a thing or two to say about that.

To treat shipowning simply as an asset-play and ignore the flow of freight rates is not dissimilar to a chain letter—if you are in it at an early enough stage and get out before the market becomes saturated you can be a winner. But for every winner there is an equal loser. Shipowning viewed solely as an asset play is a zero-sum game. Every penny which is one man's profit is another man's loss.

So it is high time that the small entrepreneurial tramp-owner changed his view and his attitude to shipping—from an asset-play to an income-flow play. If you went to a bank to borrow $5 million to finance the building of a factory in the Midlands, and instead of advancing carefully calculated cash-flow and income projections you asked for the money on the grounds that you thought the industrial property market was going up, the banker would very properly show you the door. Why then should our attitude to ships be any different? Capital investment in a ship should be amortized against a known income flow, to provide a reasonable profit for the owner's trouble. If this sort of attitude towards shipping can become the norm, if we can reduce the purely speculative element of gambling on the secondhand value of ships, then we shall be making decisive strides towards a better-balanced, less volatile, longer-term industry. If we do not, it will not be many years before we again experience the agony that we endured in the mid-1980s.

If you accept the broad thrust of this argument—that the secure future of the shipping industry depends, at least in part, on a change in attitude about where an owner derives his profit, from the balance sheet to the profit and loss account—it will be increasingly clear that a major part of the owner's stratagem will be the removal of unwanted risk. Just as any industrialist will spread his costs over a period, will use the insurance market, perhaps the futures markets to limit and control his exposure to unexpected catastrophes of one sort or another, so must the shipowner use whatever means may be at his disposal to remove unwanted risk. By doing so, he stands some chance of halting the pendulum more or less where it is.

And the futures markets do indeed have a very real rôle to play in that risk management function, in three primary areas: freight market risk, oil price risk and financial (i.e. interest rate and currency) risk.

It is the management of those three areas of risk using futures that is the main thesis of this book. Shipowners must stop the pendulum. They must adopt a more scientific approach to these three types of financial risk. And they must adopt a more sophisticated approach to some very complex financial instruments in doing so. The aim of this book is to assist them to do so.

CHAPTER 2

PHYSICAL OR FUTURES HEDGING?

What, then, are the risks, the uncontrolled nature and scientific control of which hold the key to the stabilization of a shipowner's income? There are essentially three:

(1) Freight market risk

The running costs of a vessel (manning, victualling and repair) are virtually constant, or at least are relatively easily controlled in the same way as the set costs in any business. Income earned on the ship, however, varies widely from year to year, and sometimes from month to month, or place to place. So the owner's outgoings are roughly constant, but his income from the market varies enormously. Freight market risk is the first, and arguably the most important, of the risks a successful owner must manage and control.

(2) Bunker price risk

After the fluctuations of the freight market, probably the owner's largest single area of risk exposure comes from the fluctuations in the oil price. The collapse in the 180 cst bunker price from about $200 to about $50 early in 1986 might be thought of as an unexpected windfall bonus for the shipowner, although of course freight rates quickly adjusted themselves downwards to erode it. A rise from $50 to $200 overnight might well prove catastrophic if freight rates proved to have more resistance to rising in an oversupplied market. Such a risk clearly needs to be controlled.

(3) **Financial risk**

(a) *Interest rate risk*. A ship, of course, is an enormous capital investment. Unforeseen fluctuations in global interest rates can therefore have a very profound effect indeed on the profitability (or otherwise) of trading. A contract of affreightment against a newbuilding deal which makes good sense at today's interest rate levels may well not do so five years hence.

(b) *Currency risk*. In a capital-intensive industry like shipping, which also involves gigantic cash-flows, the strength or weakness of the US dollar can be of primary importance to the success of a venture. Many of the owner's outgoings will be in local currencies, nearly all of his income will be in dollars. The currency used to pay for the ship in the first place may also be of crucial importance to the vessel's overall profitability.

The purpose of this study, then, is to consider how the shipowner can set about applying the principle of the risk/reward equation to his business. How can he limit these three primary areas of risk while still maximising his profits? In essence the solution must fall into one of two categories: Physical Hedging or Futures Hedging.

1. PHYSICAL HEDGING

How can the shipowner control these three areas of risk using what is known as "physical hedging"? In essence, this means that he lays off his risk in a physical sense elsewhere. The shipowner can, as an example:

— Take in a contract of affreightment against a newbuilding commitment (thus limiting his market risk).
— Agree a bunker escalation clause with the charterer (limiting his oil market risk).
— Agree a currency escalation/de-escalation clause with the shipyard to offset the effects of a catastrophic currency movement prior to delivery of the ship.
— Agree a forward currency contract with his bank manager to cover himself against the worst effects of a possible slump in the dollar thereafter (limiting his financial risk).

These are all examples of what is known as physical hedging. The owner is faced with a risk which he does not want, and he "lays it off"—passes it on to some other business, whether that be a bunker supplier, a shipyard or a banker—using a "physical" or "forward" contract. And by these or by a wide variety of other increasingly sophisticated physical and forward devices (swaps and over-the-counter options, for example, are becoming available in an increasingly wide variety of commodities and financial instruments), it should be possible for the shrewd owner to remove most of the more unacceptable risks of a venture.

Such devices, however, suffer from a number of disadvantages:

(1) They are really just "shifting the blister" — passing the risk on to others.
(2) A complete laying-off of risk like this would also remove most—if not all—areas of possible profit. It is the nearest commercial equivalent to putting a chip on both the red and the black at the roulette table simultaneously.
(3) They are inflexible—any change in the owner's physical ability to perform the contract (a serious delay in delivery of the ship, for example), or any change in his favour in the bunker market, or a financial windfall elsewhere, might well make any or all of these risk management devices unnecessary, or change the owner's requirements. But he will not normally be able to change their contractual details. Forward contracts of this sort are binding until they have been performed.
(4) They are unreliable—we are increasingly having to admit that few long-term commitments in the shipping industry can be considered to be 100% safe. If, for example, my prediction of a collapse to come in the dry cargo freight market is correct, how many period timecharters will suddenly be subject to re-negotiation? To the Baltic Exchange's proud motto "Our Word Our Bond" some operators should perhaps add the caveat "so long as it suits us".
(5) They can on occasion be scarce. Worthwhile period timecharters, for example, will often be hard to find. On a poor market charterers will want to fix period, but the rate which they will be prepared to pay will usually be

lower than the rate the owner could reasonably expect in the spot market in the future. And on a strong market the owner will probably want to trade the vessel spot to maximise his returns. There are, of course, occasions when it could reasonably be argued that period time charter equally benefits both parties. But for most of the time the benefits could be considered to be imbalanced one way or another. Similar arguments could be applied to long-term fuel oil contracts, even (to a lesser extent) to forward currency and interest rate deals.

When faced by a market risk the first and traditional option available to any business is the removal of that risk by a forward or physical contract of one kind or another. This is exactly what we are doing when we pay a deposit to secure a fixed-price package holiday: our risk is that either the holiday may become fully booked or that its price goes up. We hedge those risks by a forward contract with a holiday company, secured by a deposit. But what if we get 'flu the day we're supposed to fly? Or what if the price of holidays in general falls? Whatever happens, we are stuck with the pre-booked holiday.

So the removal or management of risk using forward or physical deals has a vital role to play in the overall management of a business's risk. But such deals suffer from the triple disadvantages of scarcity, inflexibility and unreliability.

The development of the concept of futures hedging as an alternative to physical hedging is designed to offer the same protection against an adverse price movement, but at the same time overcoming or avoiding these inherent disadvantages of physical hedging. How, then, does futures hedging work?

2. FUTURES HEDGING: THE PRINCIPLE

Each of the shipowner's primary areas of risk—market risk, bunker price risk, and financial risk—can now be hedged on the world's regulated futures exchanges. Market risk can be hedged on the freight futures exchange, BIFFEX, bunker price risk can be hedged on an energy futures exchange, the main two being London's International Petroleum Exchange (IPE) and the New York

FUTURES HEDGING: THE PRINCIPLE

Mercantile Exchange (NYMEX); and currency and interest rate risks can be hedged on the London International Financial Futures Exchange (LIFFE) and on the equivalent exchanges in Chicago, Philadelphia and New York.

How do futures markets address the problem of risk management, and how is the solution which they offer better than hedging using "physical" or "forward" instruments? A simple definition of a futures hedge would be "the opening of a position on a regulated futures exchange opposite to that held in the physical commodity". So a stockholder of a particular commodity protects himself against a fall in prices during the time he is holding the commodity by selling futures. A company who know that they have a futures requirement to buy a commodity (the brewer knows that he will need barley in the future, and is concerned that adverse weather conditions may drive prices up in the meanwhile) is effectively "short" of the commodity, so "goes long" on the futures market. A profit on the futures transaction will offset a potential loss on the physical deal and vice-versa.

A farmer, may, need to know the return on an acreage of grain perhaps even before he has sown the seed. He knows that he will be "long" of grain come harvest time (although of course he does not yet know the exact tonnage he will have for sale), but he has very little idea of the price he will be able to achieve on the open market at the time. He could, of course, agree a forward contract with a grain merchant to deliver a given quantity at a given price. But the disadvantage, as we have seen, of a forward contract such as this is that the farmer cannot subsequently change or escape from his contractual obligations.

The alternative would be to consider the price available on one of the regulated grain futures markets at the time he is planning his sowing. If that price is reasonably attractive, he can sell his estimated crop by going "short" on the futures market. (One of the advantages of the futures markets is that you can "sell" something you do not yet have, or perhaps more accurately buy the right to sell it at a forward date). If the grain price come harvest is actually lower than the price he has sold at on the futures market, the "loss" he makes when he sells the actual crop will be offset by the "profit" he makes on the futures side. The other side of the same coin, of course, is that if the price in reality is higher than the futures price he sold at, he will make a loss in the futures market, but a "windfall" profit in his real business—growing grain. The futures market loss he incurs is the price he pays for having the security of being able to lock in a known return on his crop well in advance of harvest. It is rather like a premium for insurance against a falling price.

By taking an equal but opposite position in the futures market to that actually held in the real physical market, the hedger achieves price protection. Whatever happens in reality—whether the price goes up, down or stays the same—the hedger will land up achieving the price locked in on the futures market.

And unlike the forward contract such a futures hedge has the great advantage of flexibility. For the hedger can buy or sell futures contracts at any time during normal business hours. Thus, if the farmer had sold 100 lots of wheat (each lot being 100 tonnes) on the London grain futures market (which indicates an expected crop of 10,000 tonnes) one day, but decided one month later that the likely crop was only 9,500 tonnes, he would simply buy back five lots at market. If it became apparent that the eventual actual price was likely to be better than that locked in, or if he achieved a physical hedge at some stage by selling his crop to a merchant, he could simply liquidate the futures hedge by buying the futures position back. Futures hedging (unlike forward contracts) provides totally flexible, easily accessible, and totally reliable price insurance.

3. FUTURES HEDGING: HOW IT WORKS

A futures market—as the name implies—is an organised formal market in which a given commodity may be bought or sold in the future (as opposed to the spot, cash or physical market where the actual commodity is bought or sold for real). In theory any commodity, financial instrument, or even service could be traded on a futures market. In the last ten years or so, the traditionally traded commodities—the "softs" (coffee, cocoa, sugar, grains) and "metals"—have been joined by a host of new commodities ranging from live hogs and new crop potatoes through the whole range of financial and stock index futures to such abstruse new suggestions as reinsurance futures and diamonds. In practice, of course, there are a great many limitations on the type of commodity which can be traded on a futures market, and very few new contracts will prove in the end to be the roaring success of, for example, the Chicago

Board of Trade grain contracts. But in theory there is no limit. How, then, do these wide ranging futures markets actually work?

At its simplest, the given commodity, financial instrument or service is bought and sold on paper at various dates in the future. Thus the farmer sells the paper equivalent of his estimated crop for delivery on the estimated harvest date at a freely negotiated price on the floor of a regulated and recognised futures exchange. The grain merchant or end user, knowing that he will in the end require the commodity, buys it. If either party to the deal does nothing else, the paper contract is converted at expiry (i.e., at the delivery date) into an actual contract, and the farmer does indeed deliver that quantity of the crop to the merchant. However, if either party changes his mind in the interim period, he can merely reverse the trade on the market much like trading stocks and shares. And in reality, nearly all futures positions are "closed out" in this way in advance of delivery because of the potential problems involved in actual delivery. (Although the hoary old story about a lay speculator arriving home from work to find his drive blocked with 500 tonnes of potatoes he had inadvertently bought is not true—deliveries are always made into Exchange-regulated warehouses.)

The fundamental principle is very simple: one party sells (goes "short" of) and the other buys (goes "long" of) the commodity, or more accurately the right to deliver or to take delivery of the commodity at some specified stage in the future. (Those who have a psychological block about "selling something which they do not have"—and that is a surprisingly common reaction—should concentrate on this concept of buying or selling the right to deliver or take delivery of the given commodity.)

The principle thus stated is not complicated. However, all traders will clearly have individual requirements—the grade of the commodity will be different from one producer to another; the exact date of delivery required by either party may be on any day of the year; the quantity required by the two parties is unlikely to match.

Now a regulated futures exchange could clearly not hope to satisfy the exact specifications and requirements of all potential hedgers. Instead, futures markets trade a standardised commodity in standard quantities for delivery on specified dates in the future. Individual hedgers merely take account of the difference between their specific requirements and the standardised product traded.

They "aim off". For example, London's International Petroleum Exchange trades a very popular Gas Oil Contract. The contract details are very specific:

Scope

Contracts will be for the future delivery of gas oil from customs bonded refinery or storage installations in the Amsterdam, Rotterdam or Antwerp areas between the 15th and the last calendar day of the delivery month.

Quantity unit

One or more lots of 100 tonnes, with delivery by volume, namely 118.35 cubic metres per lot, being the equivalent of 100 tonnes of gas oil at a density of 0.845 kg/litre in vacuum at 15 degrees Centigrade.

Specification

Gas oil merchantable quality not containing inorganic acids or halogenated hydrocarbons, and conforming to the following specification:

Specification	Units	Min	Max	Test method
Density at 15°C	kg/litre	0.820	0.855	ASTM D 1298 (in vacuum)
Distillation:	volume %			ASTM D 86
Evaporated at 250°C			64	
Evaporated at 350°C		85		
Colour			1.5	ASTM D 1500
Flash point Pensky Martens Closed Cup	°C	60		ASTM D 93
Total Sulphur	weight %		0.3	ASTM D 1552
Kinematic Viscosity	at 20°C cst		6.0	ASTM D 445 ASTM D 2500
Cloud Point	°C			
1 April – 30 September			+2.0	
1 October – 31 March			−2.0	
Cold Filter Plugging Point	°C			IP 309
1 April – 30 September			−7.0	
1 October – 31 March			−11.0	

In other words, the contract delineated by the IPE is quite extraordinarily exact and specific. Obviously, not all of those people who are using the contract to hedge their exposure to the gas oil market either use or produce oil of this exact specification. But because the contract specifications are known, they simply adjust their hedges to take account of the differences with their own gas oil. This difference is known to futures hedgers as the "basis risk".

Scientific calculation of the basis risk enables futures markets to trade highly standardised products for delivery on specific dates, which, of course, permits a fully "liquid" market. In other words, since everyone is trading a standard commodity, there will always be both buyers and sellers. And therein lies the key to the difference between the forward contract and the futures contract. The forward contract is specific in that it is tailored to the individual's requirements and it is inviolable; the futures contract is general, standardised and liquid and it can be traded in and out as often as the hedger requires.

4. HOW A FUTURES MARKET FUNCTIONS

Since all the users of a particular futures contract are trading in one standardised grade of the particular commodity, complete liquidity of trading and "transparency" of pricing becomes possible. What actually happens is that all users, both hedgers and speculators, trade through an authorised futures brokerage house. Futures brokers are represented on the floors (or pits or rings) of the various worldwide futures markets by floor traders. The floor traders congregate in brightly coloured trading jackets and by a complicated trading procedure known as "open outcry", involving a combination of shouting and tick-tack, they constantly buy and sell the commodity or financial instrument concerned. And so far as the market is concerned it is those floor traders acting on behalf of their companies who are trading. It is the futures broker who acts as principal in the market, albeit he may have a "back to back" instruction from a client. This ensures total anonymity of trading so far as the client is concerned.

5. THE PSYCHOLOGY OF FUTURES HEDGING

So futures hedging is the offsetting of a physical risk by an equal and opposite transaction on a regulated futures exchange. The farmer's physical market risk is a decline of the grain price between now and harvest time. He offsets that risk by selling futures (always, of course, taking account of his basis risk). If his fears are confirmed, he will lose money when he actually sells the harvested crop. This loss will be offset by the profit he has made on the futures market. The futures transaction should be (1) equal in size (2) opposite and (3) simultaneous. So the farmer should sell the number of lots which is exactly equal to the expected production tonnage the moment that he sows the crop (or decides to do so), and he should buy his futures positions back in full as soon as he agrees an actual physical sale with a grain merchant. He should sell his futures position "at market" (i.e., taking no notice of the level of the futures market, nor whether it is going up or down). By doing all of this the hedger has 100% price protection throughout the period of his risk exposure. That is the strict theory of the perfect hedge.

In reality, however, most hedgers are what might be called "dynamic hedgers". In other words, they will place and unwind the futures hedge at the most advantageous time on the futures market. This may not necessarily be absolutely simultaneous with their risk exposure. They may well hedge 50% or 20% of their risk exposure, and they will always try to achieve the best level for the hedge. In other words, all hedgers combine pure hedging with trading (or speculation). A simple example of this kind of thing would be a hedge which has fulfilled its usefulness (when the farmer sells the actual crop, for example). In theory the hedge should immediately be unwound at market. But in practice most hedgers will now take a view of likely movements in the futures price, trying to pick the most advantageous time to unwind the hedge. They have switched from being hedgers to speculators. It may well be that they will change the futures position back to a hedge at some later stage. In other words the dynamic hedger combines the price-fixing, insurance aspect of futures trading with the speculative trading aspects.

This fine dividing line between hedging and speculation presents most hedgers with what might be described as a psychological or accounting problem. The principle of hedging is the making of a profit on a futures exchange to offset a loss in the physical market. A properly placed classic hedge will also work the other way—an unexpected profit on the physical side will be offset by a loss on the futures side.

It could even be argued that the classic hedger should be happy to lose money on the futures market, since that itself indicates that he is actually making a "surprise" profit on his real business. Arguably, a hedger should actually want to lose money on the futures markets. However, it all too infrequently happens that way.

Many hedgers have an (understandable) mental blockage whereby they are only too happy if they make a futures profit (despite the fact that this implies a low return on their underlying business), but start to get worried if they are making a futures loss. Taken to its extreme, some hedgers will even allocate a futures profit to a particular sale or to a particular profit centre, but accumulate futures losses in some centralised sinking fund. It is amazing how many boards will lose sight of the profits when criticising (or worse closing down) the operating department which appears on paper to have made enormous futures losses.

The way to avoid this catastrophe is really a simple accounting function. Each futures trade must be allocated to a particular sale, or profit centre, or ship's voyage result. Whether that hedge makes a futures profit or loss, or breaks even, the result is then allocated to a specific piece of business. This will also ensure that the responsibility for running the hedge and taking the trading decisions will be allocated to a specific individual.

These, then, are the broad principles of futures hedging, and the broad outline of how futures markets work. The following chapters apply these principles to the three primary areas of risk for the shipowner: market risk (both dry cargo and tankers), financial risk (interest rate and currency) and bunker price risk.

CHAPTER 3

DRY CARGO FREIGHT FUTURES: THE BALTIC FREIGHT INDEX

1. THE CONCEPT OF CASH SETTLEMENT

How, then, can the principles of risk management using futures hedging be applied to the commercial market risk faced by all participants in the shipping industry? It is undeniable that the bulkcarrier freight market (with which chapters 3–5 deal; tanker futures will be discussed in chapters 6 and 7) is one of the most volatile and unpredictable of all markets. And it is becoming more widely accepted (as we discussed in chapter 1) that the violent fluctuations in the freight market are overall damaging to the shipping industry, despite the fact that some players inevitably benefit from them; and that risk management and control are an essential prerequisite of the creation of a more stable and balanced industry. Given that all of that is true, the desirability of providing a futures market in freight rates had long been obvious.

Indeed, a variety of pressure groups had been lobbying for a shipping futures market for 20 years or more before it was finally established in 1985. But the traditional wisdom had always been that such a market was impossible because of the difficulty of finding a commodity to deliver. A ship would be unlikely to be in the right place at precisely the right time. And who could guarantee that it would be? One prerequisite of a deliverable futures commodity is that it is homogeneous and readily available. Shipping quite clearly is not—it is diverse and difficult to deliver.

However, early in the 1980s, the Chicago Mercantile Exchange and London International Financial Futures Exchange (LIFFE), among others, pioneered a new concept in futures trading. When a commodity is not suitable for actual physical delivery at the maturity of the contract (as is the case with an abstract such as freight rates) an alternative is the delivery of the cash value of the commodity at that time instead.

It will be remembered that the farmer who is "short" of one lot of futures grain at the "settlement date", or date of expiry of the contract, would be required to deliver a stipulated quantity of grain of a very specific kind to whoever is "long" of that one lot of futures grain. "Longs" and "shorts" will always be equal in number and are simply matched by the Exchange. However, there is a great deal of possible inconvenience inherent in this procedure. The grain, for example, may be delivered in quite the wrong place from the buyer's point of view. This means that most futures positions tend to be "closed out" by an opposite transaction on the futures market well in advance of the delivery date. In other words, the "shorts" buy their position back, the "longs" sell it, thereby avoiding the necessity of becoming involved in the somewhat cumbrous delivery procedure.

But supposing that it was possible to deliver, or take delivery of, not a quantity of actual physical grain but of the equivalent of that grain in cash? This would give both buyer and seller full protection against an adverse price movement, but would save all of the difficulties associated with actual delivery via the futures exchange. The buying and selling of grain carries on in its normal way quite independently of, although in parallel with, the futures market. The futures market becomes in a very real sense a cash insurance market, and divorces itself from the physical business.

This move towards "cash settlement" of futures contracts was an obvious prerequisite of financial futures, trading in such things as interest rates, government stock, indexes, and foreign currencies. But cash settlement is also now coming increasingly to be used by the commodity markets as well. The highly successful Brent crude oil contract traded on London's IPE (International Petroleum Exchange), for example (see chapter 8 for a fuller explanation and description), is settled against a "Brent Index" which is produced every day by the IPE, based on reported sales of Brent Crude. This Brent Index is used as a marker for the settlement of open futures contracts on the "delivery date". And the Exchange has nothing whatever to do with the physical sale and purchase of Brent Crude Oil.

This conceptual development—of cash settlement—led to the opening on 1 August 1985 of the Baltic International Freight

Futures Exchange (BIFFEX), which trades an index of dry cargo freight rates. The "commodity" which is delivered at the settlement date on the freight futures market is the cash equivalent of the general freight market at that time as represented by this index. It is entirely a paper financial transaction, and real ships and cargoes are not involved at all. So how does it work?

2. HOW THE BALTIC FREIGHT INDEX IS CONSTRUCTED

The Baltic Exchange, the venerable London-based physical shipping exchange where shipowners, merchants and shipbrokers meet daily to "fix" or arrange cargoes for their ships, publishes a daily index of the dry bulk cargo market. This index (The Baltic Freight Index or BFI and sometimes known—quite wrongly—as "the BIFFEX Index") is similar in principle to a stock index such as the FTSE 100 index of the UK Stock Exchange, but substituting freight rates paid for the price of shares.

In constructing the index, the Baltic chose a list of broadly representative dry bulk cargo trade routes, and applied a weighting formula based on their tonne/mile importance to the world freight market. The index may change in the composition of its constituent routes from time to time, always in accordance with certain strict pre-set rules, so that it will always remain a "living" representation of the dry cargo market. The following is an outline of the current construction of the index. Further details of the historic index, and of the various changes which have occurred in the constituent routes over the years, will be found as Appendices IIA, B and C, III and IV.

The Baltic Freight Index

Route		Tonnage	Commodity	Weighting %
1.	US Gulf/N Continent	55,000	Grain	10
1a.	64000 DWAT, Hitachi Type, Transatlantic Round-Voyage			10
2.	US Gulf/Japan	52,000	Grain	20
3.	US N Pacific/Japan	52,000	Grain	7.5
3a.	64000 DWAT, Hitachi Type, Transpacific Round-Voyage			7.5
4.	US Gulf/Venezuela	21,000	Grain	5
5.	38/42000 DWAT, Delivery Continent, Trip via US Gulf, Redelivery Far East			5
6.	H Roads(option compl R Bay)/Japan	120,000	Coal	7.5
7.	H Roads/N Continent	65,000	Coal	5
8.	Queensland/Rotterdam	110,000	Coal	5
9.	Vanc & S Diego/Rotterdam	55,000	Pet Coke	5
10.	Monrovia/Rotterdam	90,000	Iron Ore	5
11.	Casablanca/W Coast India	15/25,000	Phos Rock	2.5
12.	Aqaba/W Coast India	14,000	Phos Rock	5
				100

As you can see, the Baltic Exchange have chosen those routes which are of great importance to the dry cargo market, which are not seasonal, and which are fixed (and reported) on a regular basis on the spot market. Each route is carefully defined within narrow parameters, and each route is given an individual "weighting" making it more or less important in the final calculation of the index. Until recently they were all "voyage" routes. A "voyage" rate is a per metric tonne rate payable to the shipowner by the charterer for every tonne of cargo carried from A to B, on certain pre-agreed terms and conditions. For example, the rate at the time of writing to carry 52,000 tonnes of grain loading in the US Gulf discharging in Japan is USD25.00 per metric tonne, or USD1,300,000 lumpsum. That freight rate has to cover all of the shipowner's expenses in performing that voyage. A voyage charter might be thought of, therefore, as the equivalent of hiring a taxi to take you from A to B. Time charter, by contrast, under which the charterer hires the vessel for an agreed period of time, but has great freedom (albeit within some parameters) where he trades the ship, is much more akin to hiring a car.

For the first five years of its existence, and for a complex of reasons, the BFI was composed solely of "voyage" rates. This was primarily because of the accepted wisdom that it was not possible to mix voyage rates and time charter rates in one index. But after a great deal of careful study it was decided during 1989 that sometimes the spot time charter market moves ahead of the voyage

HOW BFI IS CONSTRUCTED

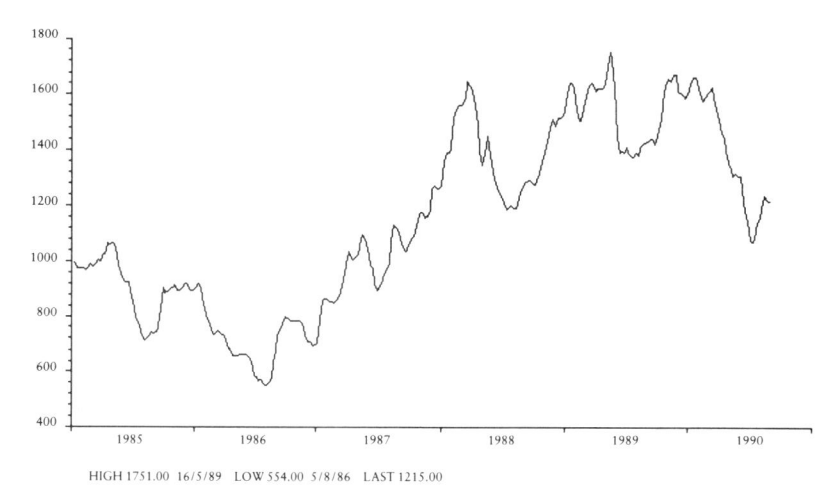

Figure 3. The Baltic Freight Index 1988/90–linear

market, and that therefore some time charter element should be included in the index. So from August 1990, an extra four time charter routes, accounting for about 25% of the total value of the index, were added.

The BFI has been compiled every business day of the year since 4th January 1985 by the Baltic Exchange, and published at 1 p.m. London time, from data supplied by a panel of leading independent London shipbrokers. The panel may vary in its composition from time to time, but is always composed of eight to twelve broking companies who are deemed by the Baltic Exchange to be of sufficient size, reputation and integrity to be good independent arbiters of the market. Each reports its view of that day's rate on each of the constituent routes. Each rate will be either an actual reported fixture, or in the absence of a fixture the panellist's expert view of what the rate would be on that day if a fixture had been concluded. Their method of reporting or estimating the rate is audited on a regular basis by an independent auditor appointed by the Baltic Exchange. Each broker reports the basket of rates to the Baltic during the morning (usually around 11 a.m.). The top and bottom rate returned for each route is discounted. The remainder are averaged and weighted according to the published formula to produce the daily index.

3. HOW THE BFI MOVES

Starting from an arbitrary "norm" of 1,000 on 5 January 1985, the index drifted lower over a two-year period (except for a little seasonal strength in late 1985/early 1986), to its all-time record low achieved on 31 July 1986 of 553.5. This level is thought by many to be the lowest level to which the freight market can possibly go; in other words the level below which there is absolutely no point at all in a vessel trading—she may as well anchor and await orders, as the current freight rates will not even cover the actual outgoings involved in a particular voyage, such as bunker charges and port costs.

From its low point in 1986, the index enjoyed a more or less straight line bull run (ignoring, for the moment, its normal seasonal fluctuations) to a peak at 1650 in April 1988. A sharp summer slump that year preceded a superb winter rally to the index's all-time high on 16 May 1989 of 1751. There was another sharp fall that summer, after which the index ambled along 50 points either side of 1600 until March 1990.

The seasonality of the index may be interesting to note from figure 4. In general the freight market moves in a fairly consistent sine curve, the high points being in April/May and October/November, the low point being end July/early August. Exceptions to this rule occur only in those years where the market is moving firmly upwards (the summer dip in 1987 was less marked than usual), or downwards (there was no spring rally at all in 1986). But by and large the index follows a remarkably predictable curve. The other rather extraordinary observation from figure 4 is the degree of "parallelism" in the index from year to year. The graph tends to follow previous years in remarkably exact "tram lines". And it is extraordinary how often the turning-point occurs on the same calendar date each year—the low point, for example, is very often the first week in August, the September/October turning-point very often after a slight dip in September.

Particular levels, too, seem to develop particular significance for the index. We have already talked about the level below which it is not possible for the index to fall; 1650 is another level which seems to have developed its own "magic". For on seven occasions the index has risen to 1650 or thereabouts, but refused to go any higher and turned back at that level. Only once so far has it breached

1650—in May 1989, and that was only for a total of a couple of weeks, and so may be viewed as an aberration. So why should 1650 be "magic"? Perhaps it is just that the freight market reaches some form of equilibrium at freight rates equivalent to an index of 1650. Perhaps the current supply of tonnage in the market will not permit higher freight levels than that. Perhaps if freight rates go higher than that it becomes increasingly difficult for commodity traders to make sales. Perhaps, for example, grain sales are switched from the US Gulf to the tonnage-rich US North Pacific.

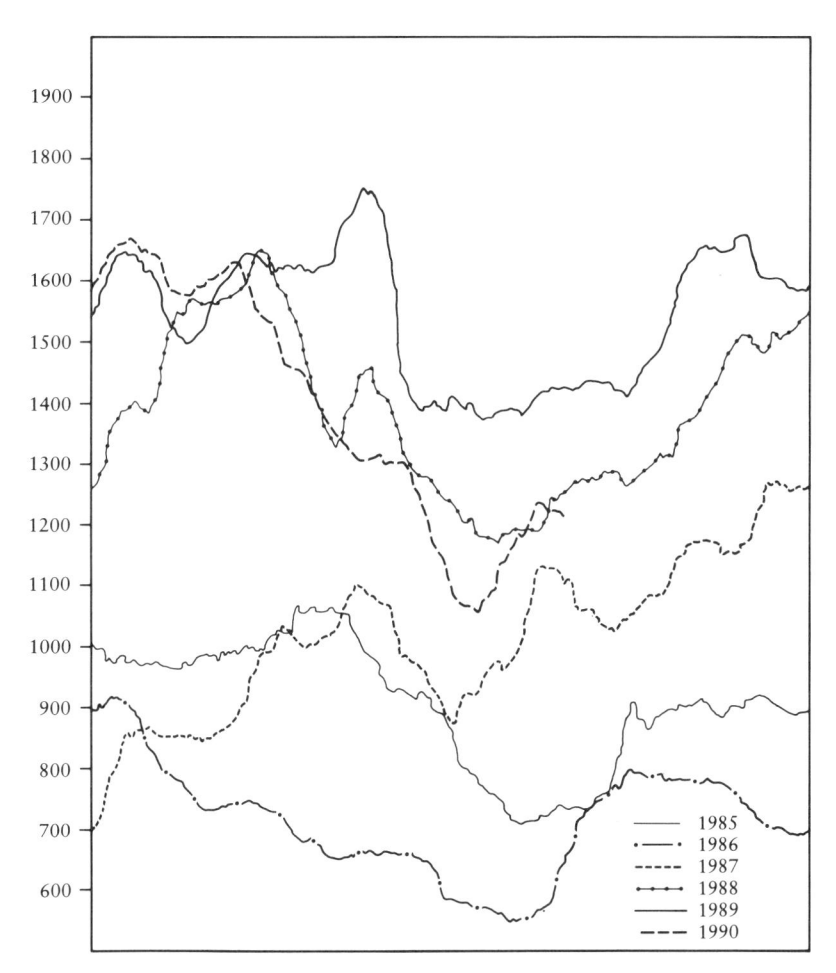

Figure 4. The Baltic Freight Index 1985/90—year-on-year comparison

Who knows what macro-economic factors may produce this 1650 sea-change? But occur it does. Too little really scientific analysis of the index has so far been carried out to be certain of all of the influences which drive it. But it would make a fascinating subject for a statistician's doctoral thesis, and after five years of life, quite enough data presumably now exists to be able to do so.

Irrespective of one's views about the exact construction of the BFI, it is probably undeniable that the index, as depicted in figure 3, is an extremely good indicator of the level, direction of change and momentum of the general dry cargo market. It is the only index produced on a daily basis and on countless occasions has proved itself to be a sensitive indicator of what is happening. There has always been a degree of debate and discussion about how it is constructed, and about particular rates on particular routes on particular days. Some argue that it is excessively panamax-orientated, too much reliant on the Atlantic trades, insufficiently representative of the handysizes or capesizes, incorrect in ignoring the time charter market for the first five years of its existence, academically incorrect in now including time charter (some argue that this is mixing apples and pears), too slow to rise and too quick to fall (or vice-versa) and the rest of it.

Shipping people tend to be contentious at the best of times, and an accurate and transparent index of what is happening in the market can be rather like a red rag to a bull. A sharply falling index belies the owner's broker's claim that "the market is holding up very nicely". A rate returned by the eight largest independent shipbrokers in London of USD $25.87\frac{1}{2}$ for 52,000 tonnes of grain to be moved from the US Gulf to Japan rubbishes the charterer's claim that the market is "actually around USD 24.00". Particularly if you accept that the shipping market is "fifty per cent fact and fifty per cent talk", the index and its daily movements will always have an important influence on the freight market, as will the published individual rates on the constituent routes. And as long as the chartering market remains the independent, argumentative, free-thinking place that it is, the index and its rates will always be subject to discussion and criticism. This comment and criticism is, to a degree, to be applauded. It keeps the panellists on their toes. It maintains the pressure on the Baltic Exchange to keep the construction of the index as up to date as it can be. And it provides an extremely useful focus for discussion about the level and direction of movement of the dry cargo market.

But discussion should never be allowed to degenerate into sterile and negative bickering. In particular, while a knowledge of and a view of the constituent routes is clearly important, and while information about changes in the rate on the more important routes may be crucial to a particular short-term trading strategy, it is entirely misplaced for a freight futures hedger or longer-term trader to become fixated by the minutiae of the index and the influences on its constituent routes. What matters both from the point of view of hedgers on the freight futures market and of general observers of the dry cargo market is the overall picture as depicted by a graph of the index such as that in figure 3. So let us get away from petty-minded discussion about the detail and concentrate our minds on the long-term picture of the market.

Another word of warning may be prudent about the BFI. Until the index was invented in 1985, the dry cargo freight market was very much harder to analyse. If you asked a shipbroker what was happening to the market, the answer would very often, and for good reason, be somewhat general, not to say hazy. But the existence of the BFI enables analysis of the market to be very much more precise and specific. "The index is close to its all-time high at 1647, that is 60 points up this week, route 2 is at USD 26.45, and going up, and Hampton Roads to Japan capesize coal is at USD 17.95" is a report which previously only the best-informed broker could possibly hope to make. Couple that analysis with information about the current level and direction of the futures prices, and you land up with a very detailed picture of the freight market.

This added clarity of vision is, of course, a very useful service to the shipping industry. But since the freight market is "fifty per cent fact and fifty per cent talk", the BFI and the BIFFEX futures prices could, if used wrongly, change from being a very useful servant into being a tyrannical master. The futures prices, in particular, will always be a great deal more volatile than the real market. If they therefore had an excessive degree of influence on the real market, they would thereby become self-fulfilling prophecies and therefore actually add to, rather than decrease, the volatility of the freight market itself.

There is a direct parallel in the stock market, where there is a current academic debate about whether stock index futures and options are a leading indicator of what is about to happen on the stock market or whether they actually create market conditions. Did they force the pace of the 1987 collapse, or did correct use of them for hedging purposes alleviate the effects of that collapse? This is a fascinating academic debate, and it is one which will go on for a very long time. And it has its lessons for the dry cargo market.

The BFI and the futures prices should only be used as a useful indicator of what is happening in the market, and as a means of insuring against adverse movements in the market. (Hedging, which will be explained in detail in the next chapter.) But they should never become the dominant influence in the freight market. The tail should never be allowed to wag the dog.

And the way to prevent that happening is by the main players in the freight market striving to take a much more detached, dispassionate and long-term view of the market than they sometimes appear to do at the moment. Shipbrokers in particular are often accused of not being able to see "further than the nose on their face". They rarely spot changes (whether up or down) in the market, and tend to have a length of vision limited by next weekend. This means that they may be unduly influenced by immediate information such as the current direction of the freight market as represented by the BFI or by the BIFFEX prices. This they must learn to safeguard against.

They must also, incidentally, learn to take a more dispassionate view of the market in general. London shipbrokers always tend to talk the market up, and to be reluctant to predict an imminent downturn. This is probably because their most important masters are the London Greek community. New York brokers, by contrast, tend to talk the market down, pandering to their main principals, the charterers. Both sets suffer from the disadvantage of the curious way in which shipbrokers are remunerated—usually by charging $1\frac{1}{4}\%$ of the freight payable. So the better job a charterer's broker does, the lower the freight rate his principal pays, and the less the broker gets. And many owner's brokers are only able to survive in a strong market, and so are reluctant to foresee or foretell a downturn. While it is well beyond the scope of this chapter, and of this book, would there not be merit in one of the many (too many) shipping "quangos" around having a look at this curious and antiquated system of remuneration, and perhaps devising some form of fee system, whereby the shipbroker is paid a fair wage for a good job done, irrespective of the level or direction of the freight market?

At all events, the BFI is now by and large accepted by most sensible observers of the dry cargo market as being a sensitive and accurate, albeit general, indicator of the market. The index itself and the data which it has generated provide a useful service to the shipping industry. Whatever one might think of hedging or trading using BIFFEX—and that is what we are now going on to explain and discuss—few would dispute that the creation of the BFI has been highly worthwhile. The shipping world should be grateful to the Baltic Exchange, and particularly to BIFFEX, for the service which the index provides.

CHAPTER 4

HEDGING ON BIFFEX: THE PRINCIPLE

1. FREIGHT FUTURES HEDGING: THE BASIC PRINCIPLE

The purpose of hedging using a futures market is the removal of an unacceptable risk. So to return for a moment to basic principles, it is perhaps worth reiterating the risks which we are trying to remove. The basic risk for the shipowner is that the market will decline between now and the time that his ship or ships are "open" (i.e., empty of cargo and looking for the next business). The basic risk for the charterer is that the market will strengthen between now and the time that he needs to move his cargo, thus wrecking his budgets and removing his profits. So how do they respectively set about insuring themselves against that happening using freight futures?

Their risk is analogous to the farmer and the brewer. The farmer's risk is a fall in the price of grain, the brewer's vice-versa. Both of them can neatly and efficiently remove and manage their risk by respectively selling or buying grain futures. If you substitute an index for the standardised parcel of grain, and you substitute cash instead of actual delivery of the commodity, you have index futures trading.

In BIFFEX, instead of buying or selling a standardised parcel of grain or currencies the freight futures user buys or sells the Baltic Freight Index for a set forward date. This concept of buying or selling an index may seem foreign to you, but it is a futures broker's everyday currency. For example, if I were to ask for estimates of the number of people attending the cup final, I might say that I was a buyer at 70,000 for 1p a head, a seller at 80,000. If someone else thought 80,000 was too high we might trade at 75,000—me being the buyer and him the seller. We would be making a market in the number of people likely to attend the match. By doing so, we are creating our own informal futures market—fans at the match being the commodity traded, 1p per head being the value. In the event 76,000 people attended the 1990 cup final. Had I bought at 75,000 I would have made a 1000-people profit or £10. The seller would have settled by paying me the £10. Similarly you can buy or sell the Baltic Freight Index at certain stipulated forward dates, depending on whether it seems to you to be too high or too low.

The shipowner sells the BFI for a specified forward date, the charterer buys it. The price at which they respectively sell or buy it is set by a process of free and open negotiation on the floor of BIFFEX.

For example, imagine that the BFI today (1 March 1990) stands at 1600. The price presently being traded on the freight futures market for April 1990 is 1700 (indicating that more than a 6% increase is anticipated in the dry cargo market between now and the end of next month). Our owner (or his bank) is of the view that a 6% improvement over that period is well worth locking in, so he sells April futures at 1700. Similarly, July 1990 is presently trading at 1320, indicating a nearly 20% decline April to July, or a $17\frac{1}{2}$% relative decline over today's market. Our charterer (or his treasury department) takes the view that that is a fundamentally cheap price and he is concerned that he may well pay more than the equivalent of 1320 to move his July cargoes. He buys the index at 1320 for July.

We will go on later to discuss in very much more detail how the owner and charterer work out their hedges. But the principle should be clear: if the owner wishes to ensure a certain level, or fears that the physical freight market will go down and so erode his profits, he sells the index at specified future dates. If the charterer wishes to ensure a certain level, or fears that the market will strengthen against his position, he buys the index. The owner is "long" of tonnage, so he goes "short" of futures. The charterer is "short" of tonnage, so he goes "long" of futures. Both parties offset a risk exposure in the real physical market by an equal and opposite (and usually simultaneous) paper transaction in the futures market.

How, then, might these simple hedges work out? The owner sold April futures at 1700. His view of the market was correct, and by the time his ships are "open" in early April the spot index is standing at 1600, so he fixes the ships at lower levels than he had hoped but at the level he had been expecting. However, because he had sold at a futures price of 1700 he can now buy back his futures position at 1600, making a 100 point profit. That profit will offset the "loss" he is making on the ships.

What would have happened if his view (that a BFI 1700 was more than he could expect to achieve) was actually wrong? Suppose, for example, that by the time he fixed his ship, the index stood at 1800? In this case, the owner will be making an unexpected windfall profit on his ships, since the market is actually 100 points higher than the futures market's expectation had been when he placed the hedge back in March. However, since he sold the futures at 1700, he now has to buy his position back at 1800. He makes a loss of 100 points in the futures market, which removes the unexpected profit he has made on the physical market. In other words, by selling freight futures at 1700, he is locking that level in whether the market goes up, down or stays the same. Come hell or high water he will land up earning the equivalent of 1700 index points. The same argument, except in reverse, applies to our hypothetical charterer's hedge.

So hedging using the freight futures market is a method of locking in a predetermined cost or return, whatever subsequently happens to the market. It is an insurance policy against the more damaging fluctuations in the freight market.

2. FREIGHT FUTURES HEDGING: THE SIMPLE STRATAGEM

The principle of freight futures hedging, thus explained, may seem simple and straightforward enough. The practice of planning a hedging stratagem, calculating the level and size of the hedge, placing the hedge on the futures exchange, keeping track of it, and eventually unwinding it, is a good deal more complicated. It is a mistake, perhaps, to try to oversimplify freight futures hedging—it is one of the most sophisticated (and some would say difficult) concepts to arrive in the shipping industry since the invention of steam. Let us look, then, at each of these stages in more detail, starting with a consideration of the hedging stratagem.

The owner or charterer is faced with a position of risk exposure the moment he becomes long (or short) of tonnage. For whatever reason, he finds himself with a cargo and no ship to carry it or vice-versa. His risk is that between that moment and the time that he actually fixes a ship, the freight market will move against his

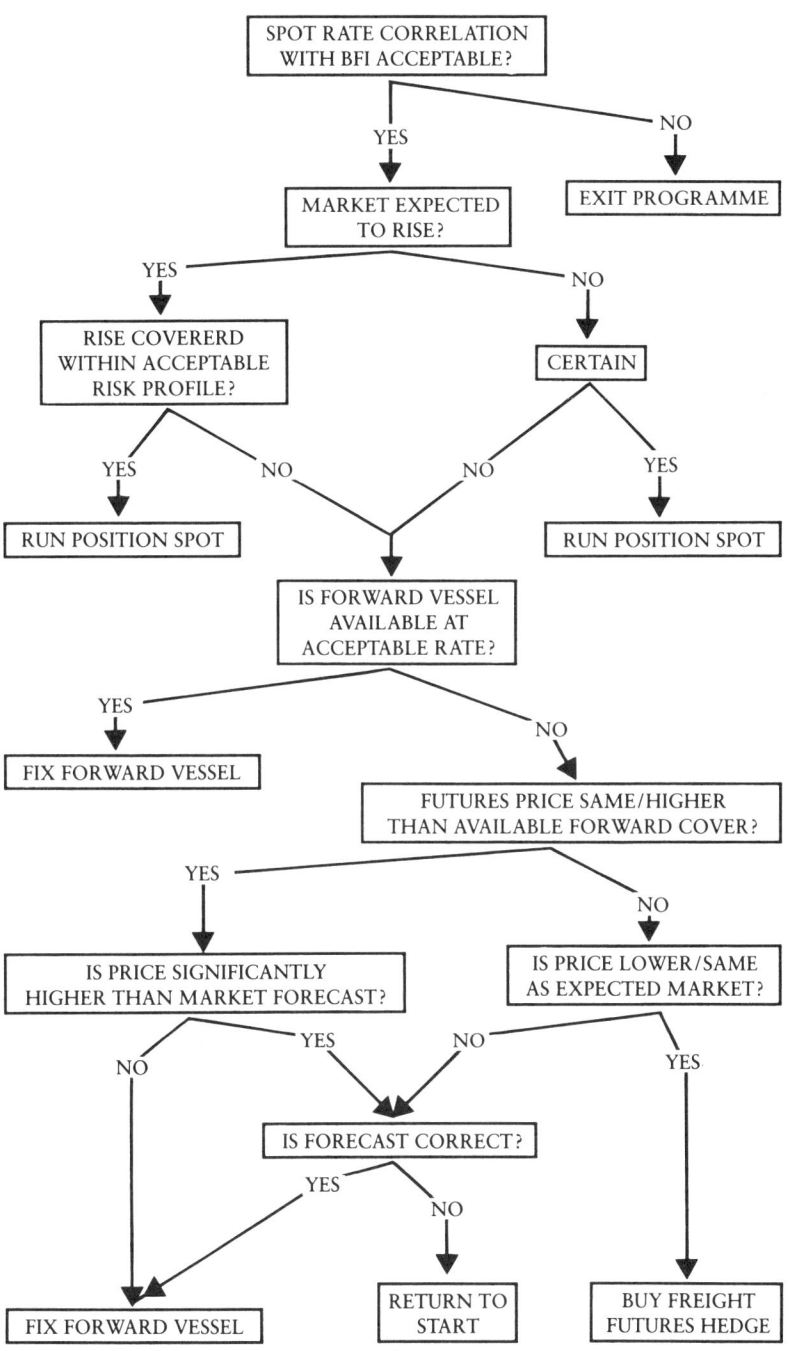

Figure 5. Charter's decision-making process

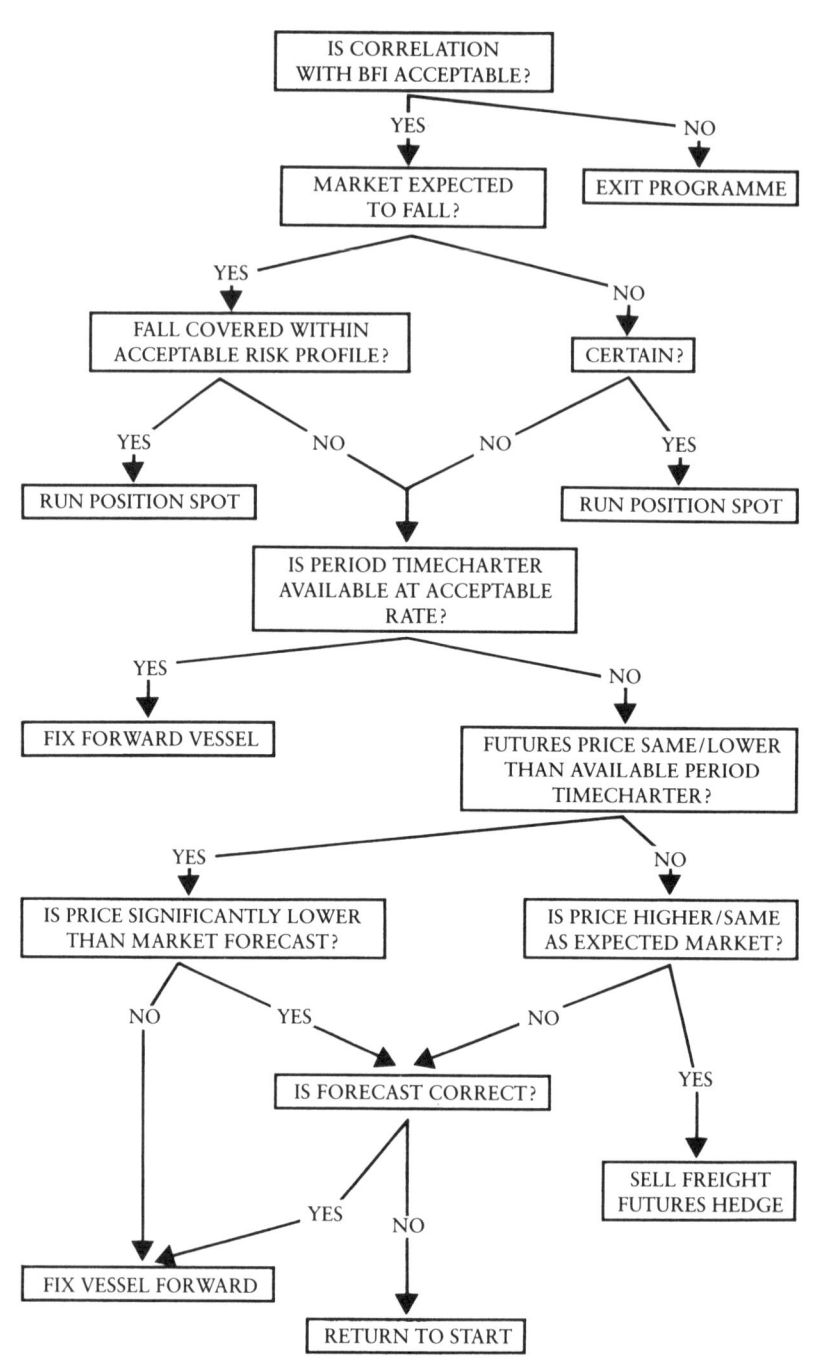

Figure 6. Shipowner's decision-making process

THE SIMPLE STRATAGEM

position. At that moment, the potential hedger has to make a number of decisions.

He can: (1) run the risk exposure closer to the shipment date, or (2) fix a ship or cargo on the forward market if one is available at the freight rate required, or (3) take a suitable hedge on the freight futures market.

So the potential hedger has to take a number of commercial decisions: whether to fix the ship forward, whether to run the cargo spot or whether to take cover on the freight futures market. How does he make these decisions?

The first stage is also the easiest—he goes on to the freight market and discovers whether forward cover is available, and if so at what level? He then ascertains the freight level available on the futures market, compares the two rates and acts accordingly. In other words, there are always two alternative markets—the real forward market and the paper futures market. So the key to the successful use of the futures market will be the ascertaining of the level offered by BIFFEX as opposed to the level offered on the forward freight market.

The answer will probably mostly be a combination of futures cover, forward cover and spot risk. The exact mix will depend on market conditions and the attitude of the particular shipowning company to risk. But at the end of the day all companies involved in the shipping industry (on either side) should land up with a "risk portfolio" specifying the degree of risk acceptable, and from that should be able to calculate a hedging stratagem—how much of that risk they must lay off elsewhere, and how.

The steps involved in the evaluation of freight market risk, the systematic calculation of an acceptable "risk profile", and the decision-making process of how to lay off or control unwanted risk is best explained as a flow diagram such as figures 5 and 6. But assuming that the result of that decision-making process is to use the freight futures market to lay off risk, then the "simple hedging stratagem" is quite straightforward. As a charterer you buy freight futures at the moment of your risk exposure; as a shipowner you sell freight futures. You run the futures position until your risk exposure is removed (i.e. you fix a ship), at which stage you unwind the futures position on the market. Any profit on the futures side offsets a disappointing fixture. A loss on the futures market indicates a better-than-expected voyage result.

3. FREIGHT FUTURES HEDGING: SOME DEVELOPMENTS AND REFINEMENTS OF THE SIMPLE HEDGING STRATAGEM

This basic hedging principle can be developed into a variety of more or less complicated hedging stratagems. Individual hedger/traders will quickly develop their own methods with experience. However, as a general guideline, the following are a few slightly more sophisticated applications of the basic principle:

(1) The expansion hedge

Freight futures can be used as a mechanism for expansion. An operator who is offered a contract of affreightment for ten cargoes, but whose normal risk portfolio would allow him to take only five, would probably previously have had to decline the contract. He can now lay off the unwanted five cargoes using freight futures. Similarly, the freight department of a trading house working within a "risk ceiling" can now expand that ceiling by hedging.

(2) The positioning hedge

Freight futures can be used as an aid to flexibility. An owner who anticipates the market moving in his favour in the next month or two may well nonetheless not wish to take the risk of running his ships dead spot. By taking out a futures hedge he has removed the risk and can sleep easy in his bed, while continuing to watch the market until he sees the level he needs. When he fixes (whether spot or forward), he unwinds his freight futures position.

(3) The basis hedge

A charterer and shipowner may both wish to fix a given very forward position, but be unable to agree a rate because they hold opposite views of what the spot market will be at that time. But it may be that they would prefer to know that they have suitable tonnage or cargoes under their belts. They can now break the deadlock by fixing fully firm, all terms and details agreed, except the rate. The rate can be based on a formula derived from the spot index at the time of shipment. Both parties will have the security of knowing that the voyage will be performed, and both know that they will neither pay nor receive more (nor less) than the spot market at the time of shipment. And either (or both) of them can take out an appropriate freight futures hedge.

(4) The blanket hedge

A charterer or shipowner who has freight exposure evenly spread over the year may well not know in precise terms which cargoes or ships he needs to hedge. But he has a broadly-based exposure over a long time. Where previously he might, for example, have taken tonnage on time charter or fixed a contract or affreightment as a general hedge, he can now buy (or sell) futures contracts evenly spread over the year. A large charterer, for example, could buy say 100 lots of each of the dry cargo futures contracts on offer as a general "blanket" hedge.

These and other more complicated hedging, trading and arbitrage stratagems enable the charterer and shipowner to control their freight risk. The analysis of a risk portfolio and the development of a hedging stratagem will become second nature to the experienced hedger. It should indeed become as natural as any normal freight market negotiation, and of course will already be familiar to most sophisticated freight market operators.

The scientific calculation of an acceptable risk profile and the careful planning of a suitable hedging stratagem is the essential prerequisite of successful use of the freight futures markets.

CHAPTER 5

HEDGING ON BIFFEX: THE DETAIL

THE CALCULATION OF THE DRY CARGO FREIGHT FUTURES HEDGE

A properly worked-out hedging stratagem such as that described in chapter 4 will give the hedger a general idea of the risk which he wishes to remove and of the way he wishes to do so. Let us now assume that he has concluded that a freight futures hedge is the most suitable avenue to hedge the particular risk he has in mind. In chapter 4 we were talking very much in generalities. But at this stage in his thought process, the hedger will have to become a good deal more specific. He will have to work out (no doubt in co-operation with his futures broker) the size, level and detail of the hedge. There are several elements in this: (1) the various details of the traded contract, (2) correlations between his particular trade and the BFI, (3) the level of the hedge, and (4) the size of the hedge (for both voyage and time charters).

Let us look at each of these in some detail.

(1) The contract

All futures markets including BIFFEX trade a standardised commodity. The individual hedger must therefore adjust his hedge to take account of any differences between the standardised futures contract and his particular requirements. A hedger on BIFFEX is buying or selling an index of the general level of freight rates at a specified future date. He must therefore consider carefully any differences between the contract traded (the generality of the freight market) and his own particular requirements.

(a) The contract month

First of all, because of the necessity of finding matching buyers and sellers, it is not possible to trade all of the dates of the year. If the hedger could stipulate the precise date for which he wished to place a hedge (presumably the date on which the ship or cargo is open), it would be extremely unlikely that he would find another hedger with the equivalent (but opposite) requirement. Instead, the market stipulates certain dates (the last day of the "contract months") for which it is possible to place a hedge. BIFFEX trades the four "quarterlies" — January, April, July and October—up to two years ahead. In addition it trades the "spot" and the "prompt" months—i.e., this month and next month. For example, on 1 January 1991 the "board" of traded months would look like this:

Spot:	Jan 1991
Prompt:	Feb 1991
Nearby Quarterlies:	Apr 1991
	Jul 1991
	Oct 1991
	Jan 1992
Distant Quarterlies:	Apr 1992
	Jul 1992
	Oct 1992
	Jan 1993

On 31 January (if it is a business day) January ceases to trade, February becomes the "spot" month, and a new March contract is introduced as the "prompt". A full table of contract availability will be found as Appendix V.

The fact that only certain months are offered is a necessity of all futures trading. But it should not be a substantial inconvenience to the hedger. Freight being a long-term business, it should not be difficult for the user to decide which one or more of the contract months to use. If a vessel is coming open at the end of January or mid/end April, the choice is not difficult (use January and April respectively). If the vessel is coming open during February, it is likely that the January contract will be the one to use. Sometimes it might be best to place half of the hedge in January and half in April. The hedger uses whichever contract month is either (a) closest to the position, or (b) more convenient

Figure 7. Comparative chart of BIFFEX prices

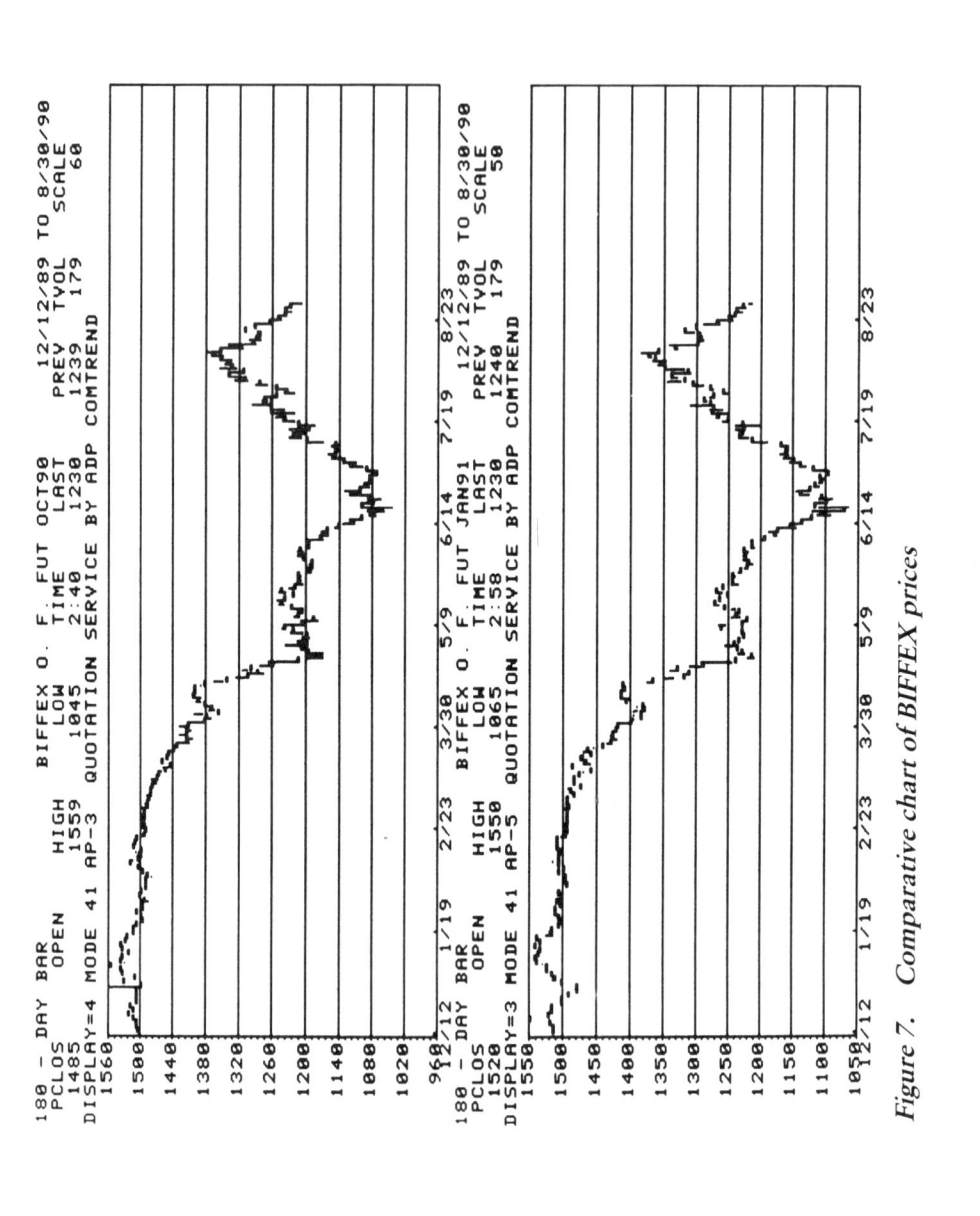

CALCULATION OF DRY CARGO HEDGE

for some other reason, or (c) seems in the commercial judgement of the hedger or his futures broker to be offering a better hedging opportunity. Skilful use of the "spot" and "prompt" months in particular offers great flexibility in the way the hedge is constructed.

One feature of all futures markets is that the "distant months" (in the case of BIFFEX those more than 12 months away) tend to be illiquid—in other words rather thinly traded. At first sight this makes a long-term hedge difficult to place. So a particular type of trading stratagem known as "rolling over" may be necessary to place a large-volume hedge. This stratagem is possible because of a phenomenon observed in most futures markets—that all of the months tend to trade in parallel with one another. We do not need to go into too much detail about why this should be, but the charts of two BIFFEX months (figure 7) demonstrate that it is indeed the case. Let us suppose, then, that a perfect hedging plan may involve selling 100 lots of each of the first eight contracts, but it is only possible because of the lack of liquidity in the long months to do so in the first four. The solution is to sell twice the quantity in the first four (200 in each instead of 100). Then, as the nearest contract becomes spot, you can close out the excess 100 lots, reopening the position in the first "distant" month. "Rolling over" is the best possible graphic description of this operation.

(b) The contract value

The hedger on BIFFEX buys or sells a multiple of "lots". Each lot is worth the index price (let us say 1495 for April 1990) × $10. Thus each April lot is worth USD 14,950 of freight cover. This aspect will be discussed further below.

(c) Other contract terms

"The Last Trading Day" (the last opportunity to trade a particular contract) is the last business day in that delivery month.

"The Settlement Day" (on which the Clearing House settles all outstanding contracts) is the first business day after the last trading day.

"The Minimum Price Movement" ("Tick size") is one index point, which is equivalent to $10 per lot.

"The Settlement Price" is the average of the last five daily indices. (This method of using an average to calculate the settlement price reduces the possibility that a powerful player in the spot or futures markets could influence the settlement price.)

These, then, are the details of the contract between the willing buyer and willing seller on BIFFEX. A consideration of each of these terms—particularly the contract months available—is the first stage of the potential hedger's calculation of how to use freight futures hedging. The second stage concerns the degree of correlation of his particular trade with the BFI.

(2) Correlation with the BFI

The quoted price on BIFFEX is an index based on a basket of freight rates. The prices therefore suffer from the same disadvantage as all indices—they reflect the general movements in the freight market very well, but may or may not be an accurate reflection of the particular route or vessel to be hedged. It would be very misleading to claim that all types of ship and cargo in all parts of the world can be hedged on BIFFEX with the same degree of accuracy and ease. The Baltic Freight Index is, primarily, Atlantic-based, panamax-based and grain-based. So the panamax owner trading the Atlantic dry cargo spot market (particularly Transatlantic or Gulf/Japan grain) is in a very strong position to take out a very accurate hedge indeed.

At the other end of the scale, a charterer who requires an overage tweendecker in the Mediterranean would have to think very hard before using the market. Between the two there is a whole range of tonnage portfolios, some of which are more precisely hedgeable than others. The success of the hedge will depend on the degree of correlation between the Baltic Freight Index and the trade or fleet in question.

There are, of course, a number of highly sophisticated statistical ways of assessing correlations. Using a computer, a statistician will be able to assess standard deviations, calculate "Beta factors", the "theta" and "gamma" and the rest of it. Statistical analysis of this sort, developed for use particularly in arbitrage trading against stock indexes, certainly has a role to play. And the more sophisticated a view the potential hedger can take of the correlation between the particular risk to be hedged and the BFI, the better.

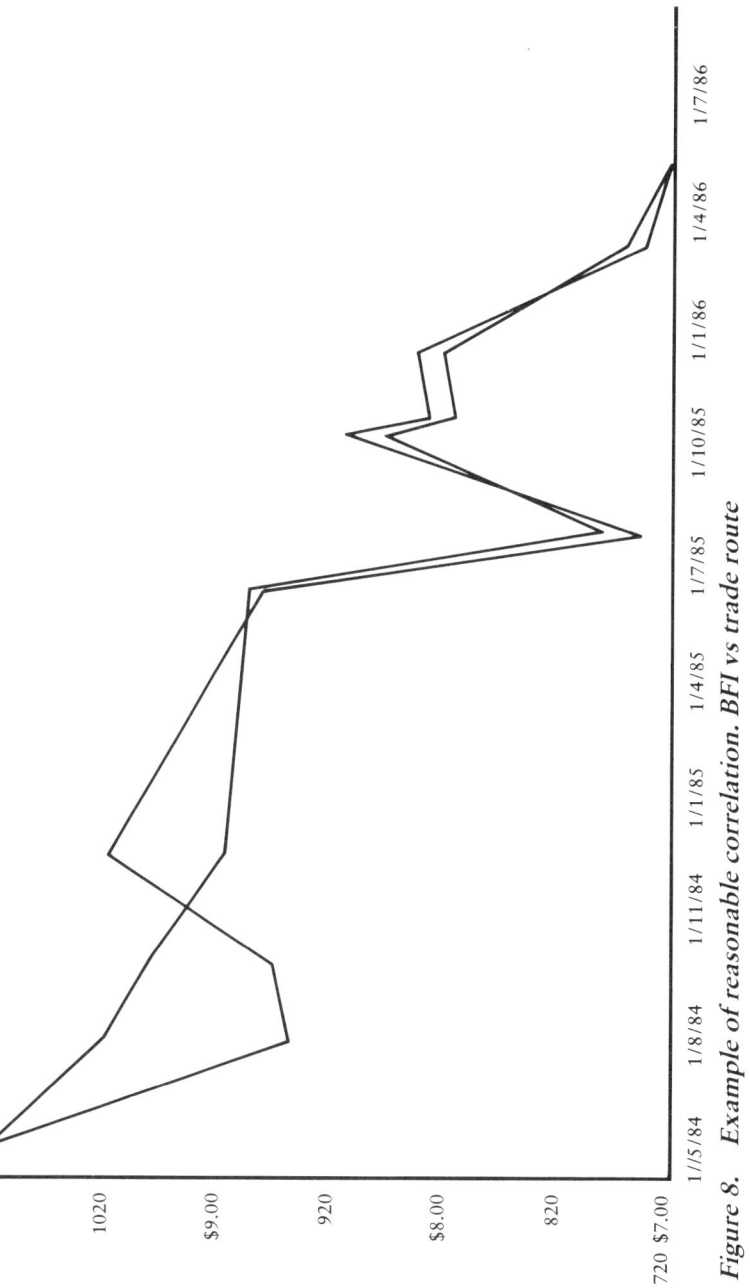

Figure 8. Example of reasonable correlation. BFI vs trade route

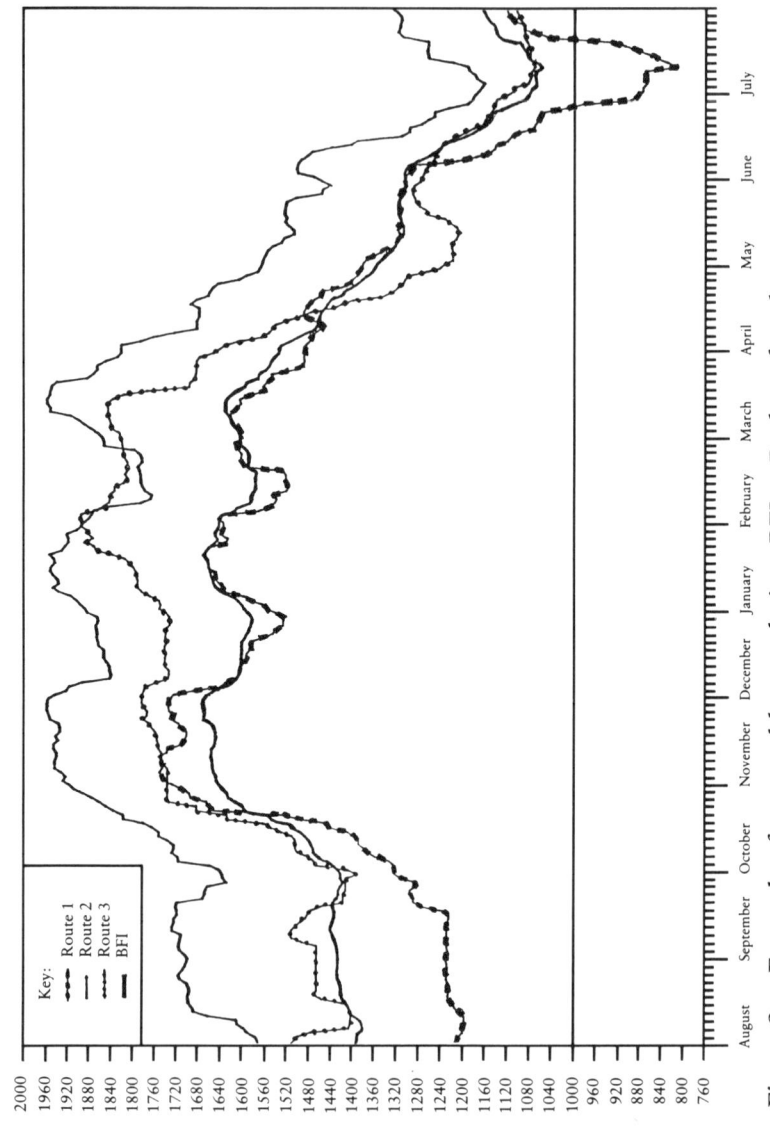

Figure 9. Example of reasonable correlation. BFI vs Basket of trade routes

CALCULATION OF DRY CARGO HEDGE

But an excessive degree of accuracy in the calculation of correlations, and the resulting great accuracy in calculating the size and the level of the hedge (see below), is, in my view at least, fundamentally misleading. For the freight market is a difficult and hard-to-define market (compared, at least, to the Stock Exchange where each price is known to the last penny on a second-by-second basis). Freight Futures hedging is by definition a comparatively imprecise mechanism—more of an art, it might be said, than a science. It is therefore a mistake to allow oneself to be fooled by convincing-sounding statistical analysis resulting in a very precise "correlation coefficient" and a very detailed hedging plan. A much more sensible approach seems to me to be what might be described as "visual correlation analysis".

If the hedger supplies historic data of the rates actually paid on the route to be hedged over as long a period as possible, his BIFFEX broker will be in a position to draw graphs (either manually, or more often using a computer) which will show at a glance what sort of correlation (or lack of it) exists. The graph will look something like figure 8. It will be seen that this trade (which is Pacific-based) had a poor correlation with the BFI in the first half of 1985, but had quite a remarkably good correlation in the second half. Figure 9 demonstrates the same thing for a basket of routes. Graphs such as these are really all that are needed to calculate the hedger's correlation. Those pundits who have tried to introduce such abstruse subjects as Beta factors and relative volatility indicators are in danger of confusing (if not misleading) their clients. A good visual correlation should be quite enough to assess the viability of the hedge.

The aim of such a visual correlation should be to come up with an answer along the following lines:

1. My trading pattern has a good/reasonable/poor/hopeless correlation with the BFI in terms of volatility. (25/50/75/100% higher/lower.)
2. My trading pattern has a reasonable correlation, but there is a time difference of 1/2/3/4 weeks.
3. On the basis of 1 and 2, I should adjust my hedging programme as follows: buy/sell X% more/fewer lots than necessary of previous/subsequent/more than one contract month.

This exercise is certainly a useful one, and certainly one which all potential hedgers should attempt in conjunction with their broker. However, three important points should be borne in mind on this question of correlations.

First, no hedge on BIFFEX (whether an owner's or a charterer's hedge) will be absolutely precise. If the hedger loses, for example, $100,000 on a particular position as a result of the physical market moving against him, freight futures hedging will probably compensate him for something between say $75,000 and $125,000. But at all events it is better than having no compensation at all.

Secondly, in broad terms—in other words looked at over a period of months rather than days—the Baltic Freight Index can be shown to have a reasonable correlation with almost any type of ship trading almost anywhere in the world. So although detailed work on correlations is obviously helpful, most hedgers will probably find they have a reasonable "broad-brush" correlation.

And thirdly, it is possible to think of BIFFEX in terms of catastrophe insurance. Most businesses—including shipowners and charterers—are well used to writing a small percentage into their budgets to cover normal adverse freight market movements. What they are unable to cover while still remaining competitive are the large unexpected movements to which the shipping market is subject. Freight futures can protect a hedger from those movements. His correlation may not be very good, particular hedges may not work out in detail, but for a very small premium, the hedger is protected against disasters. None of us complain if we come to the end of the insurance year without our houses having been burgled or our cars written off, despite the fact that we have "lost" the insurance premium. In some respects the same attitude should apply to freight futures hedging.

Having considered the contract details and the degree of correlation with the index, the next stage is to calculate the level and size of the hedge required.

(3) Calculating the level of the hedge: voyage charters

We have so far discussed in some detail why freight futures are needed, and how BIFFEX can be used to remove freight market

CALCULATION OF DRY CARGO HEDGE

risk, some of the hedging stratagems which can be employed, some of the pitfalls to be avoided, and the framework within which the hedge can be constructed (contract details and correlations). We have not so far addressed the "nuts and bolts" of freight futures hedging at all. But this is a subject which can no longer be delayed.

The underlying contract being traded, of course, is the Baltic Freight Index. The futures prices on BIFFEX are also expressed as an index. For example, the BIFFEX prices may look something like this:

(Closing prices on 19/1/90)

Contract	Close	PR Close	High	Low	Vol
BFI	1668	1669			
APR 90	1655	1677	1670	1655	85
MAY 90	1645	1673	1664	1644	197
JUL 90	1664	1687	1681	1664	170
OCT 90	1410	1425	1420	1410	54
JAN 91	1510	1515			
APR 91	1508	1518			
JUL 91	1518	1538			
OCT 91	1335	1335			
JAN 92	1540	1540			

In other words, compared to a spot index of 1668 the sum total of the views of the future trend of the freight market of those actually trading on BIFFEX currently indicate a general expectation of a small decline by February 1990, a further fairly steep 200 point decline by the summer, some recovery in the autumn and so on. The prices move up and down depending on the buying or selling pressure in the market at any one time. The "bid" and "offer" column give an indication of the level at which traders are willing respectively to buy and sell the forward month in question. In exactly the same way as we discussed making an informal futures market in the number of people attending the cup final (bid at 75,000, offered at 80,000, traded at 75,000 and eventually settled at 76,000 meaning a 1,000 point profit for the buyer), BIFFEX users buy or sell the index at these stipulated forward dates.

But how do you make more sense of these index figures in real terms which can more readily be understood by the shipping industry as a whole? Relating BIFFEX futures prices to reality is currently thought by many to be the key to the more generalised use of freight futures.

There are essentially three main ways of relating the BFI and the futures prices to reality:

1. By direct proportion.
2. By looking at historic equivalence.
3. By means of a variety of short-hand quick calculations.

Let us have a look at each of these methods in more detail.

(a) The direct proportion method

Since the futures prices are simply a function of the spot index, they can be viewed as a percentage increase or decrease over spot. The spot index is a reflection of a particular spot rate on a particular route, so that the rate implied on that route by a particular futures price can be calculated by simple direct proportion.

Thus if the spot rate for the route to be hedged is, for example, USD10.00 per metric tonne, and the spot index is 1,000; and if the futures price for next April is 1,100 (i.e., 10% more than today's spot index), the implied rate for next April (assuming a reasonable correlation with the index) is USD11.00. In other words:

$$\frac{\text{Futures Price}}{\text{Spot index}} \times \text{Spot rate} = \text{Implied Future Rate.}$$

This will be the fastest and most easily-used method of calculating the implied rate in the future for the route to be hedged. It can be developed by the individual user in a variety of ways to suit his own uses, but the principle is very straightforward.

(b) The historic rate method

Since the BFI and the rates on its constituent routes have been published on a daily basis since 4 January 1985, and since during that time the index has fluctuated from a low of 550 to a high of 1750, historic information about the equivalence between the index and particular freight rates is available for almost every

CALCULATION OF DRY CARGO HEDGE

conceivable freight market level. By sampling those freight market levels from the historic data published by BIFFEX, it is possible to create the hedger's own "freight futures ready-reckoner" along the following lines:

BIFFEX Price	1. Gulf/ Holland	2. Gulf/ Japan	3. Nopac/ Japan	4. Gulf/ Venezuela
600	5.00	8.05	6.50	5.50
700	5.55	10.00	7.00	6.75
800	6.30	12.25	7.40	9.20
900	8.00	13.50	7.90	10.40
1,000	10.00	16.00	8.60	11.50
1,100	11.00	18.30	11.50	12.50
1,200	11.80	20.00	12.30	13.50
1,300	12.60	21.70	12.90	14.50
1,400	13.60	23.33	13.10	16.00
1,500	14.60	25.00	14.40	17.33
1,600	15.60	26.70	16.40	17.70
1,700	16.60	28.33	17.50	18.00
1,800	17.60	30.00	18.50	19.00

Notes:
1. Gulf/ARA 55,000 HSS, 11 DAPS
2. Gulf/Japan 52,000 HSS, 11 DAPS
3. USNOPAC/Japan 52,000 HSS, 11 DAPS
4. Gulf/Venezuela 21,000 HSS, 4 days/1,000

The difficulty with this approach to freight futures is that it assumes that all freight rates rise and fall exactly in parallel with one another and with the index. This, of course, is far from the truth. The relative strength of particular freight markets may well vary wildly from time to time. So while the calculation of a "ready-reckoner" such as this on one's particular route or trade is a useful guide to approaching freight futures hedging, it should always be used with a certain amount of care. Before relying too heavily on it, the hedger must ascertain that the particular route in question has not for any reason moved "out of line" with the generality of the freight market as represented by the BFI.

(c) *The quick estimate method*

Use of the futures market should eventually become familiar to you as an everyday part of your trading operation. You are likely eventually to trade into and out of the futures market all day, every day. When this happens you will inevitably develop your own methods of calculating the real value of the futures prices. These methods will be more or less sophisticated depending on the individual and the trade concerned, but will inevitably include elements of the direct proportion method and the historic rate method, probably coupled with your own short-cuts. For example, as a good rule of thumb the rate for transatlantic panamax grain can be converted to an approximate BFI level very easily by adding one to the dollar figure and dropping the decimal point. So a transatlantic grain rate of, say, US$7.65 is roughly the equivalent of BFI 865. BFI 1,235 is roughly the equivalent of $11.35 for transatlantic grain.

Similarly, Gulf/Japan Panamax grain has fluctuated over the years more or less in line with the BFI. This knowledge permits one to calculate the ratio between the two, which in the case of Gulf/Japan comes out at roughly 60. This figure is calculated simply by dividing an average of indexes, by an average of several Gulf/Japan rates. This figure may vary by a factor of perhaps 10%, but it nonetheless gives a good general guide to the real meaning of the BFI or of a futures price. Simply divide any index figure by 60 and you have a rough guide to the Gulf/Japan equivalent. Figure 10 uses this quick estimate method to convert the closing futures prices on 7 February 1990 into Gulf/Japan equivalents.

		Futures prices C.O.B. 7/2/90	Approximate Gulf/Japan equivalent
BFI		1588	25-55
Feb 1990		1554	25-06
Mar 1990		1582	25-52
Apr 1990		1600	26-67
Jul 1990		1343	21-66
Oct 1990		1540	24-84
Jan 1991		1498	24-16
Apr 1991		1515	24-44
Jul 1991		1343	21-66
Oct 1991		1540	24-84
Jan 1992		1575	25-40
Average	1990	1524	24-75
	1991	1474	23-78
	Overall	1516	24-32

Figure 10. Futures prices and Gulf/Japan equivalents

CALCULATION OF DRY CARGO HEDGE

This is not the correct place to suggest more of these rough and ready methods of estimating an equivalent rate. Each individual will quickly develop his own methods. But the exercise of quick and reasonably accurate conversion of a per metric tonne rate to an index figure and vice versa is clearly central to the successful use of freight futures hedging.

(4) Calculating the size of the hedge: voyage charters

The hedger on BIFFEX buys and sells a multiple of lots, each lot being worth the index price times $10 in terms of freight cover. So a futures price of 1450 gives freight cover of US$14,500 per lot. How does the hedger decide how many lots to buy or sell?

First he calculates the per metric tonne rate which the futures market is indicating, using one of the methods described in section 3 above. For the sake of the example, let us use the direct proportion method.

1. Today's spot rate	$10
2. Today's BFI	1,000
3. Futures price (April)	1,100
4. Implied future rate	$11.00

The charterer has a grain cargo of 60,000 MT to move next April. His lumpsum freight exposure is therefore 60,000 × implied future rate of $11.00 = $660,000. Each "lot" is worth the futures price times $10. By dividing the lot value into the lump sum implied freight exposure, you calculate the number of lots to be bought.

5. Implied freight exposure	$660,000
6. Lot value (1,100 × $10)	$11,000
7. Lots to be bought (line 5 divided by line 6)	60

So, to lock in a rate of $11.00 for next April, the charterer buys 60 lots of April futures. (This would be a 100% cover—the charterer may well decide he needs less than that, perhaps 50%, in which case he would buy 30 lots).

All of this can be boiled down into a proforma worksheet in the following form:

The voyage hedge calculation worksheet

Cargo Size:	% correlation with BFI
Loading Port:	% of risk to be hedged
Discharging Port:	Time correlation with BFI
Load/Disch Terms:	Freight element in CIF price
Lay/Can:	

1. Today's rate	$	PMT
2. Today's BFI		
3. Futures price for date to be hedged		
4. Implied future rate (line 3 ÷ line 2 × line 1)	$	PMT
5. Implied freight exposure (cargo size × line 4)	$	
6. Lot value (line 3 × $10)	$	
7. Lots to be bought/sold (line 5 ÷ line 6)	+/−	Lots
8. Adjusted for correlations	+/−	Lots

Regular use of this worksheet will confirm the principles involved in the hedger's mind until the various steps become completely automatic. The principle of the hedge may sound complicated when read in detail, but should be reasonably straight-forward when laid out like this. In essence, the level which the futures market is offering is calculated by direct proportion. To lock that level in, you buy or sell the number of lots calculated by dividing the lumpsum implied freight by the lot value (price × $10).

(5) Calculating the level of the hedge: time charters

The use of freight futures presents one immediate problem for the shipowner which is not faced by the charterer. When considering their future risk exposure owners tend to think in terms of a daily hire rate, rather than a per metric tonnage voyage rate. So the owner must equate the daily return he requires to something which can be understood in freight futures terms, and equate the index and futures prices back to a time charter equivalent.

This can be done in one of two ways.

(a) The voyage estimate method

Using the experience and expertise which he has built up over the years the owner can equate the daily return which he requires to the equivalent voyage rate on any of a number of representative

CALCULATION OF DRY CARGO HEDGE 59

trade routes (such as Gulf/Holland, Gulf/Japan or North Pacific/Japan panamax grain, all three of which are major components of the index), and then hedge that rate on the futures market.

However, in calculating the time charter rate to voyage rate equivalence, the owner must take a view of how such things as bunker prices, draft restrictions, port and canal dues and currency exchange rates will move in the period between now and the time that the ship is open. A change in any or all of these factors will affect the PMT voyage rate and therefore the BFI, but they will not necessarily affect the time charter equivalent to the same extent (or under some circumstances they may even have the opposite effect). The owner may incidentally consider hedging his bunker, foreign exchange or interest rate exposure using the futures markets. This is described in chapters eight and nine.

(b) The rule of thumb method

If the owner is unwilling to go through the laborious and by definition subjective exercise of equating the daily return needed to a voyage rate which can be hedged on BIFFEX, he can use what might be called the rule of thumb method.

A time charter rate is effectively the net return on a given voyage, the voyage rate is the gross return. An owner calculates the difference between the two all the time in the normal course of his business. A particular voyage route is offering US$ X PMT. Does that equate to the time charter rate he needs, or can he see a better time charter rate elsewhere? The owner should be so familiar with the individual characteristics of each ship (particularly her speed and consumption), with that ship's normal trading pattern, and with normal port and canal dues to be expected in that trading pattern, that he should be able to calculate the time charter to voyage rate equivalence very easily. It is often said that many owners do so on the floor of the Baltic Exchange on the back of a bus ticket, although nowadays most larger owners have computer programmes which do it for them.

This exercise becomes even easier using an index. For example, the difference between net and gross returns on a standard non-economical panamax vessel trading mainly in the Atlantic at current bunker prices is about 300 index points (i.e., of the 1600 index points in the spot BFI, rather less than one-fifth is made up of bunkers, port and canal costs). It will be larger than 300 points (perhaps up to 500) for a handysized vessel, where bunker costs and port dues probably represent a larger proportion of the gross freight. It will be lower (perhaps down to 200) for an economic panamax type. Any owner should be able to work out quite easily for each of his ships what index figure represents the difference between gross and net returns. For the sake of this example we will use our standard panamax with a gross/net difference of 300 index points.

This means that when the BFI is at 1,500, the owner's time charter equivalent index (i.e., the index of net returns on the ship) is around 1200. When the BFI is at 1400, the time charter equivalent index is at 1100 and so on.

Detailed analysis of time charter rates over the last five years against the index indicates a reasonable degree of correlation between the two. (And inclusion of time charter rates in the construction of the index from August 1990 should increase the closeness of that correlation.) The six month time charter rate expressed in US dollars per day over that period can be shown to be higher than this time charter equivalent index by a factor of 10.* (Again rather smaller than that for handysizes, rather larger for capesizes.)

So as a very good rule of thumb it is possible to calculate the time charter equivalent of a BFI (or a futures price) by subtracting 300 from the index and multiplying by 10.

Thus, when the index is at 1,500 the equivalent time charter rate for an Atlantic-based non-eco panamax is $12,000. When the index is at 1,700, the time charter rate is $15,000.

Particular owners will be able to refine these figures with regard to particular ships in co-operation with their BIFFEX broker. In general terms, it is remarkable how well it works.

(6) Calculating the size of the hedge: time charters

Using this rule of thumb method, it is comparatively easy to calculate the hedging level being offered by BIFFEX at any given moment.

*I am indebted to Michael Hampton of Chase Manhattan Bank for pointing this out.

CALCULATION OF DRY CARGO HEDGE

Owner A has a 60,000 DWAT B/C with average fuel efficiency coming open in the Atlantic in April 1991, which he is considering hedging on BIFFEX. The vessel is worth US$14,000 per day on today's market, and today's BFI is 1700.

Vessel: m/v *BIFFO*
DWAT: 60,000 mt DWAT/41's.w.   % correlation with BFI: Good
Speed and consumption: 13/33 (1,500) % risk to be hedged: 100%
  + 2½ MT DO   Time correlation with BFI: Reasonable
Period to be hedged: 1 April/31 May 1991

Line 1	Today's approx T/C rate	US$14,000
Line 2	Today's approx BFI	1,700
Line 3	Time charter equivalent index (1700-300)	1,400

April is presently trading at 1,800. Using the rule of thumb method, he quickly calculates that this is the equivalent of $15,000 per day (1,800 − 300 × 10), which he feels to be an attractive rate.

Line 4	Futures price	1,800
Line 5	T/C equivalent (FP − 300 × 10)	= $15,000

He wishes to hedge at that level for a 60-day period, the centrepoint of the period being end April. He wishes to lock in the $1,000 per day difference between spot and implied futures time charter rate (line 5 − line 1), times 60 days, or $60,000.

Line 6	Difference to be hedged × days	= $60,000
Line 7	Difference between BFI and futures price	= 100
Line 8	Lot value, line 7 × $10	= $1,000
Line 9	Owner sells	60 lots

It may sound complicated, but it is really a very simple drill which simply needs to be learned. It is summarised in the following time charter hedge calculation worksheet.

The time charter hedge calculation worksheet

Vessel: m/v Biffo   % correlation with BFI: 100%
DWAT: 60,000 MT DWAT/41'ss   % of risk to be hedged: 100%
Speed and Consumption: 133/33 (1,500) + 2½ DO   Time correlation with BFI: Exact
Period to be hedged: 1 April/31 May 1991

1. Today's approx time charter rate	$14,000
2. Today's BFI	1,700

3. Time charter equivalent index (spot) (line 2 − 300)*	1,400
4. Futures price for date to be hedged	1,800
5. Time charter equivalent 10* × (line 4 − 300*)	$15,000
6. Difference to be hedged (line 1 − line 5) × No of days	$60,000
7. Difference between BFI and futures price (line 2 − line 4)	100
8. Lot value (line 7 × $10)	$1,000
9. Number of lots to be bought/sold (line 6 divided by line 8)	− 60
10. Adjusted for volatility	− 60

*These figures apply to average panamax vessels. They would have to be adjusted for other types of vessel.

This is, of course, a very simple example of a straight hedge. By selling 60 lots of April futures at 1,800 or better this owner is guaranteeing himself a daily return of about $15,000 per day. If the ship earns less than that, because the freight market does not rise, his loss will be compensated by a profit on the futures market, when his contracts are settled out at the end of April.

Exactly the same principle can be applied to a broader "blanket hedge". For example, if the owner wishes to hedge the vessel over the next two years (in other words to achieve the same end result as a two-year time charter but with the great commercial advantages of reliability and flexibility), he would sell 120 lots in each contract month at 1,800 to achieve the equivalent of $15,000 a day.

However, because of the normal seasonal fluctuations to which the shipping market is subject, it is very unlikely that he will be able to do so. It is very much more likely that the futures prices over the two-year period he needs will look something like this:

DRY CARGO HEDGING 63

Futures contract	Futures price	Approx T/C equivalent
Jan	1,841	$15,500
Apr	1,860	$15,500
Jul	1,602	$13,000
Oct	1,715	$14,000
Jan	1,810	$15,000
Apr	1,806	$15,000
Jul	1,525	$12,700
Oct	1,740	$14,500

So four out of the eight contracts are offering him a lower return than he requires. Three of the remaining four are offering him exactly what he wants, and the last is offering him $500 per day more. Realistically, he must aim to average 1,800 or better over the two-year period. So instead of a straightforward hedge, selling a set number of lots of a particular contract to remove a particular risk, the owner combines the skills of trading with those of hedging. He aims to build up a portfolio of short positions roughly equivalent to his risk by selling those contracts which offer the best return. The owner's risk is generalised (most charterer's risks are specific), so he places a generalised hedge. In this example, he will probably immediately sell 120 January and April, and perhaps half of his total requirements in the July, Oct and Jan, in the hope that the market may subsequently improve, in which case he will be able to raise his average.

DRY CARGO HEDGING USING BIFFEX

The potential hedger may by this stage feel a little shell-shocked. For it is true that some of the concepts and details explained in this chapter are fairly complex, and may seem foreign to a degree to many freight market operators. And it is necessary in a textbook such as this to go into some detail about exactly how the market operates. But the fundamental principles of using BIFFEX for hedging purposes should not be lost sight of, and are comparatively straightforward. The shipowner faces the risk of the market going down, the charterer risks the market going up. They respectively sell and buy freight futures. If their worst fears are realised and the market does indeed move against them, a freight futures profit will offset a physical market loss. The opposite equally applies—that an unpredicted favourable movement in the freight market will result in a freight futures loss.

Slightly more complicated is the calculation of the equivalence between the BFI and futures prices and the real freight market, and the calculation of the number of BIFFEX lots to be bought or sold to offset the risk. But in the event neither of these calculations is nearly as complicated as might appear. As the index becomes more and more familiar, the significance of its movements will become more and more obvious. And the level and size of a freight futures hedge will probably more often be directed in reality by the level and liquidity of the futures markets, and by the hedger's "feel" for the way the market is moving than by any purely mechanical mathematical calculation. In other words, there is a close connection between speculation or trading on the market and hedging. Owners will sell BIFFEX when they perceive the current prices to be too high. Charterers will buy it when it seems too low. Their futures activity will always be a suitable combination of hedging and trading.

CHAPTER 6

TANKER FREIGHT FUTURES: THE 1986 EXPERIMENT

It may seem strange that we have concentrated entirely up to this stage on the dry cargo bulkcarrier market. For while the bulker is the workhorse of the dry cargo market, and while the bulkcarrier market is demonstrably volatile and demonstrably in some need of an effective freight risk hedging mechanism, dry cargo freights constitute less than half of the world's annual shipping bill. By far the largest single sector of the chartering market is, of course, in tankers—both crude oil and products. This apparent omission is really for two reasons. First, apart from a brief experiment with tankers during 1986, the only freight risk management tool available to the shipping industry has been the BIFFEX dry cargo contract. And second the nature of the oil tanker industry has until now precluded a freight futures contract. In the 'sixties and 'seventies so much of the oil market was controlled first by the "majors" and then by the "producers" in the form of OPEC (including as late as the early 'eighties by means of the so-called "net-back arrangements", which effectively removed the buyer's commodity price and freight rate risk) that there was neither need for freight futures nor a sufficiently large number of players in the market to ensure its liquidity.

What is more, any successful launch of a brand new futures contract needs a good body of interested participants to pump in a little activity and liquidity from the first day of the new contract to generally "get it going". The world's major grain trading houses—Cargill, Dreyfus, Bunge and the like, together with such bodies as the Grain and Feed Trade Association (GAFTA), the Baltic Exchange and the London Commodities Exchange (now renamed London FOX), were prepared to perform this function of "priming the pump" before the launch of the dry cargo contract in 1985, just as the major sugar houses had done for the relaunch of the London Sugar Terminal Association in 1957. The grain traders needed freight futures. They could hedge their commodity deals in Chicago and London, but the only available means of laying off freight risk was by the clumsy and inefficient "physical hedges" such as period time charter or Contracts of Affreightment. The freight element was a very significant part of the CIF (Commodity, Insurance and Freight) price of grain. The CIF price of US wheat in Japan at the moment is roughly $145, of which freight accounts for $25 or 18%. A very slight fluctuation in the freight market, a dollar or two either way plays havoc with the sale, so that control of the freight market is an all-important part of trading in grain. Indeed, it is arguably the most important part of grain trading, as it has such an important effect on the margin. So the invention of freight futures was an important development for the grain houses, and one that they were more than ready to support in full.

But at least until fairly recently, the oil trading world was rather different. In the mid-'eighties, when crude was trading at over US$30, a freight element of 50 cents or so was pretty insignificant. A 10 cent fluctuation one way or the other was of course important to the shipowner, and of some significance to the end user or buyer for whom every cent counts, but when trading margins might be as fat as a dollar or two, freight market fluctuations were comparatively insignificant to the trader.

This lack of a dedicated body of users determined to see the futures market succeed was amply demonstrated in 1986 when BIFFEX briefly flirted with tanker futures in an experimental form. The mistake BIFFEX made was to think of a contract and then to try to sell it to a reluctant industry. The oil industry's reluctance to adopt "TIFFEX", as it was known by some, was compounded by the fact that it was launched on 1 February 1986—exactly the time when the crude price was collapsing from a high of US$35 or so to a low of US$8 or thereabouts. If you were long at that time you had more to worry about than freight rates. And if you were short you were laughing all the way to the bank. In either case a futures broker attempting to explain the merits of freight risk hedging using futures was probably not a particularly welcome visitor.

Moreover, not only were physical market conditions unpropitious, not only were the oil companies—still comparatively unsophisticated in their approach to the use of futures in general at

THE 1986 EXPERIMENT

that time—reluctant brides to say the least, not only were the futures brokers fully occupied with developing the dry cargo market, and therefore perhaps reluctant to devote the time and resources necessary to marketing tanker freight futures sufficiently to make it fly, but also it should perhaps be admitted with hindsight that the contract offered was not ideal for hedging purposes.

Using the dry cargo contract as its exemplar, the tanker futures market traded an index composed of key tanker routes, reported on a daily basis to the Baltic Exchange by a panel of eight London tanker brokers. The composition of the index was as follows:

Route No	Cargo Size	Trade	% Weighting
1	50,000	Venezuela to New York	12
2	65,000	Sullom Voe to Marcus Hook	10
3	80,000	Sullom Voe to Rotterdam	16
4	80,000	Libya to Fos	15
5	80,000	Red Sea to Genoa	8
6	80,000	AG (ex Iran/Iraq) to SE Asia	10
7	130,000	East Coast Mexico to Rotterdam	5
8	130,000	Bonny to Rotterdam	14
9	130,000	Sidi Kerir to Fos	10
			100

The charts (figures 11 and 12) indicate the projected index back to 1984, and the actual index in 1986.

The main details of the contract were as follows:

Contract	Baltic Tanker Index Contract.
Unit of trading	Baltic Tanker Index valued at $10 per full index point.
Trading months	The spot month, the two subsequent months and the next three quarterly calendar months.
Settlement	Each month of the year.
Settlement day	The second business day after the last trading day.
Last trading day	The last business day in the month (excepting December which is to be the 10th day or if not a business day the previous business day).
Minimum price movement	0.5 index points ($5 per lot).
Settlement price	The average of the index on the last trading day and the two previous working days.

The difficulty with the contract was two-fold. First, its very volatility was a problem. It is always said that a prerequisite for a

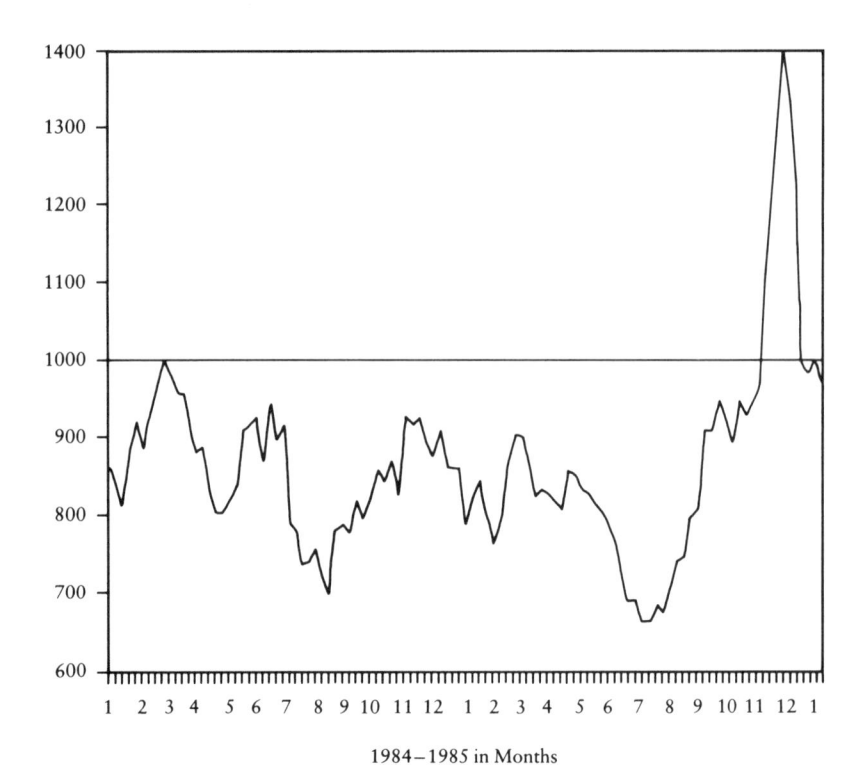

Figure 11. *Baltic Tanker Index 1984–1985*

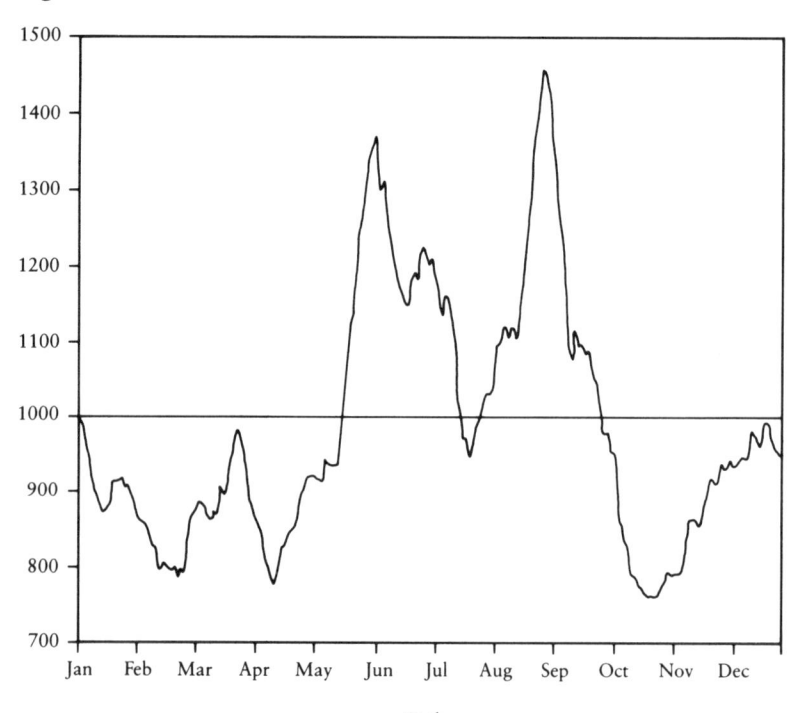

Figure 12. *Baltic Tanker Index 1986*

successful futures contract should be volatility. And that is certainly quite true in the sense that if a commodity's price is flat and predictable, then there is clearly no point in using a futures market either to protect yourself against an adverse price fluctuation or indeed as a speculative investment. So some volatility is clearly necessary. But violent and unpredictable (and largely unexplainable) volatility of the kind experienced by the tanker index during 1986 (the cash index rose 500 points, or 50% in the first two weeks in August and then collapsed 700 points by mid-October) is really too much for any market—futures or physical—to handle.

That is particularly true with a cash settlement contract such as BIFFEX, since there are no "natural" buyers and sellers to slow down the movement of the futures prices. In other words, since farmers are *always* interested in selling grain, albeit trying to achieve the highest possible price, and brewers in our example *always* need to buy it, there will always be players on both sides of the grain futures market. More sellers than buyers means that the price goes down, more buyers than sellers means that the price goes up. But there will always be some players on both sides of the market creating liquidity even in very volatile trading conditions. But where you are trading an index, there are no natural buyers and sellers, except at those times when it is entirely unclear which way the market is going. The freight market goes through long periods of this kind of uncertainty, but when it "breaks out" and starts a move either upwards or downwards there is usually no stopping it. It becomes obvious to all involved in the market what is happening, and the freight market is after all 50% fact and 50% talk. This "one-way market" effect was even worse in the tanker freight futures market—once a move started it tended not to look back, it "went down without even touching the sides", as one floor trader described it.

So an index-based futures contract in something as volatile and as abstract as tankers was never likely to succeed. One prerequisite of a successful futures contract is a close link between the futures prices and the underlying "cash market". This is particularly achieved by means of arbitrage between futures and cash. The relationship between cash and futures in a "physically deliverable" futures market, such as grain, should be:

$$\text{Futures Price} = \text{spot price} + \text{carrying cost}$$

The carrying cost is the cost of warehousing the commodity plus the interest cost of financing it between now and the future delivery date.

In other words, if the futures price is higher than the spot price plus the cost of storing and financing the commodity in the intervening period, you can buy the cash commodity and sell the futures, thereby locking in a risk-free arbitrage profit. The "cash and carry", as it is known, is one of the most important principles of futures trading.

But when the cash commodity is as complex as space on a ship, even worse when it is an index based on a total of nine different freight rates, there is no possibility at all of efficient—or at least of straightforward or obvious—arbitrage between spot and futures.

Some sophisticated operators, it is true, have experimented with arbitrage against the dry cargo futures market, and with some success on occasion. But bearing in mind that a successful arbitrage of this kind involves not only a suitable futures transaction but also the chartering of a ship, it is clear that only the most sophisticated of operators could do it.

All of this meant that the 1986 experiment with tanker futures could not be a success. The extreme volatility of the index, the lack of the cash/futures link or of realistic arbitrage possibilities, the comparative insignificance of the freight element in the CIF price of oil, the oil industry's natural fixation with the collapsing commodity price, an absence of natural market makers, and a comparative lack of sophistication in futures terms within the oil and the tanker industry, all of these things militated together in 1986 to remove any hope of launching a successful contract.

In the next chapter we will examine why these circumstances are different in 1990, and why there is a good chance of success for an entirely new freight futures contract in tankers.

CHAPTER 7

TANKER FREIGHT FUTURES: THE 1990 CONTRACT[1]

Unlike the 1986 experience, when BIFFEX thought of a contract and then tried to sell it to an unwilling oil and tanker industry, the industry and in particular the oil traders approached BIFFEX during 1989 to request that they re-examine the concept of tanker futures. For many circumstances have completely changed since 1986. First, the oil price has stabilised (at US$20 per barrel, plus or minus two or three dollars). Freight currently represents roughly 5% of the price of crude, 10% of the price of products and the traders operate on very much thinner margins than they ever have in the past—often as little as 20 cents a barrel. All of this means that even comparatively insignificant fluctuations in tanker freight rates could have potentially disastrous consequences for the trader's transaction. Freight rates have developed a sharply higher significance, particularly for the oil trader, than they have had before. And there is no efficient and readily accessible way of hedging or offsetting that freight risk. Chartering a ship is by definition clumsy and expensive, particularly if, as is so often the case, the trader is holding the particular cargo for a very short space of time.

Increasingly sophisticated traders can hedge their price risk on the world's fast-developing oil futures exchanges (the use of which will be explained and discussed in full in chapter 8), but there is absolutely no way at all that they can remove their freight market exposure. And that they do not like. But a

1. The Iraqi invasion of Kuwait and the resulting political crisis in the Arab Gulf, which occurred in the week that this book was sent to the publishers, seems likely once again to produce a very strong oil price, and the possible concomitant of a reduced importance of the freight element in the CIF price of crude oil. The launch of a tanker contract has therefore been delayed until after the Iraqis withdraw.

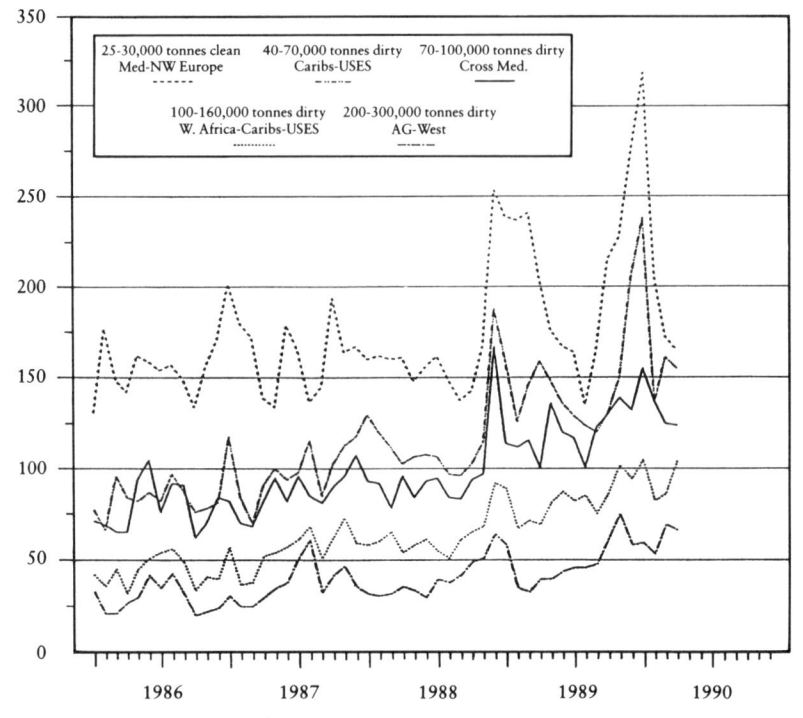

Figure 13. Tanker spot rate trends

redesigned freight futures contract might offer them a neat and efficient way of laying off their freight market risk.

The statistics for the supply and demand of tanker freights of which the following is a summary, and which will be found in graphic form as figures 13 and 14, highlight the need for tanker futures.

Tanker supply

— Fleet declined from peak 332 million tonnes deadweight to 232 million deadweight (30%), 1978/1988.
— Although orders for newbuildings are at a high level, the old age profile of the fleet necessitates an extensive renewal programme.
— Scrapping is now at a minimal level, the second-hand price is high.

THE 1990 CONTRACT

— Despite claims that it is economically possible to extend the life of the current fleet, increasing special survey costs, increasing safety and pollution concerns, and vastly better fuel efficiency of modern ships all combine to make fleet renewal more attractive than life extensions.

Tanker demand:

— Demand is directly allied to: OECD demand for crude oil
: OPEC crude price
— Total Non-Communist World Oil Production (46.3 million barrels per day) is now at its highest since 1980.
— Non-Communist World Oil Consumption is estimated at 50 million barrels per day, and is increasing every year.

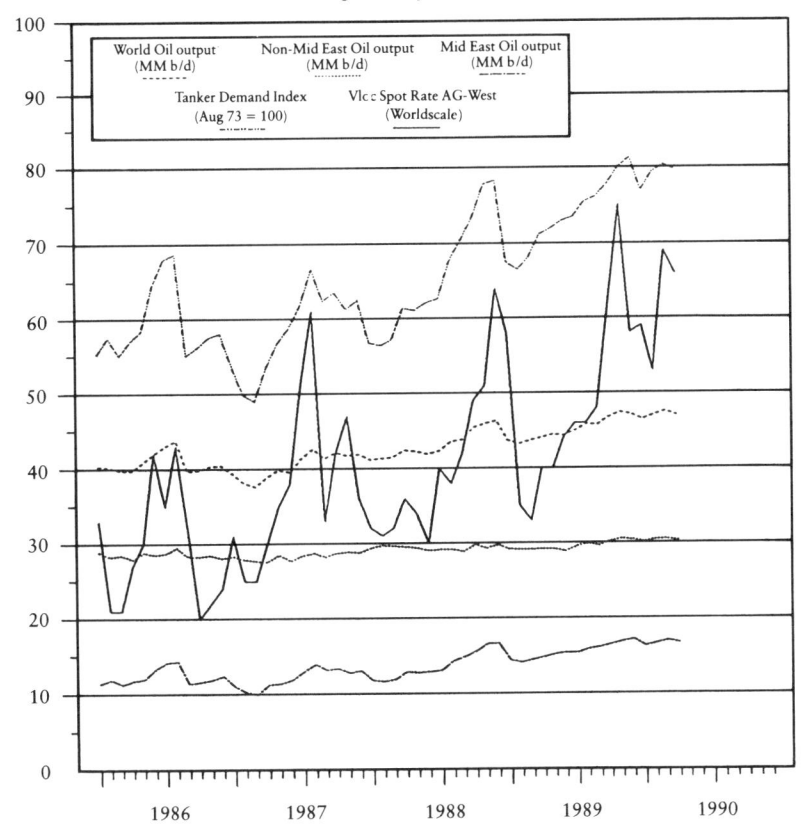

May 1990 Source: Drewry Shipping Consultants Ltd.

Figure 14.   Oil output and tanker demand

World seaborne oil trade:

— After a sharp decline in volumes moved by sea from its peak in 1979 (1,487 million tonnes) to a low of 871 million in 1987, volumes have once again grown to an estimated 1,000 million tonnes in 1989. The sheer volatility of these volumes is in itself interesting.

— Rather more than half of the 1989 volume (perhaps as high as 60%) was carried in single voyages (compared to 1973 when only 10% of oil was shipped on a spot basis). This reconfirms the dependence of both charterers (traders) and shipowners on the spot freight market. 416 million tonnes of crude oil is now fixed on a spot basis per annum, compared to 323 million tonnes in 1983.

Balance of tanker supply and demand:

— The rise in demand and decline in supply noted above has produced a substantial reduction in inactive tonnage within the past couple of years. In other words, the tanker market is now much closer to supply/demand equilibrium than it has been for many years.[2]

Tanker freight rates:

— The main influencing factor is supply and demand as outlined above. Since the supply side is inelastic, demand for crude oil transportation (which of course is closely allied to the price of crude, with a possibly inverse correlation) is the primary influencing factor. Tanker freight rates in general are extremely volatile, probably much more so than the underlying oil price.

---

2. I am indebted to Mr H. Song, then an MSc student at Plymouth Polytechnic, both for re-igniting my interest in tanker futures and for supplying much of this statistical analysis in his unpublished MSc thesis entitled "Tanker Freight Futures". His enthusiasm, and mine, was ignited by that doyen of shipping studies, Professor David Moreby, of the Institute for Marine Studies at Plymouth Polytechnic, to whom the shipping industry as a whole—whose thanks are too often unspoken—owes a debt of gratitude.

— The oil majors' control of the oil price was replaced in the early/mid 'seventies by OPEC. OPEC control of the crude price has itself declined since then, although major interruption to the supply of OPEC crude (e.g. the 1990 Gulf Crisis) would still be crucial.
— This has resulted in a much greater importance for the spot market, and for the traded (as opposed to the term) market.
— This increased usage of the spot market, the majors' declining control of the oil price, and of the tanker market, and an increasing tendency toward supply/demand equilibrium in the tanker market, has meant a greatly increased importance of the freight rate. Freight rates are now so volatile that they significantly affect the traders' narrow profit margins. And all of the indications, coincidentally from the supply side and the demand side, suggest a huge increase in tanker (particularly VLCC) freight rates and volatility in the next year or two.

In a word: tanker freight rates are highly volatile and look like becoming more so in the next year or two, freight rates are developing an ever-increasing significance for traders, and there is no efficient hedging mechanism currently available. The stage seems set for the introduction of freight futures.

A series of interest groups and industry committees discussed the subject of tanker futures in 1989, and came to the conclusion that it would be the wrong approach to try to create an index of different tanker freight rates such as had been attempted in 1986. The trouble with the index approach was that by attempting to be all things to all men and to reflect the generality of the spot market, it accurately reflected nothing at all. There was an insufficient correlation between the old index and any particular freight route. It was extremely difficult to "identify" with an index. It was therefore generally agreed that a preferable approach would be to trade one well-known "yardstick" of the tanker industry as a whole, the obvious one being the VLCC movements from the AG to the West, or West Africa to the US Gulf, 130,000 size.

The disadvantage of this, clearly, could be that charterers or owners who are primarily involved in other trades or sizes might dismiss the contract as being irrelevant to them. But at least by being entirely clear what the futures market is trading, particularly if it is a widely-accepted yardstick route such as VLCC AG/West, many different participants would be able to use it, "aiming off" to take account of the differences between that trade and their own. A close study of the correlation between the traded route (for which the historic data is obviously available for a long way back) and one's own route very quickly provides a clear conclusion as to whether the futures contract can be used or not.

So one route rather than an index it was. But how to ensure fair and accurate settlement of contracts which remained "open" at settlement date? It will be remembered that ICCH settles open dry cargo contracts at a cash price calculated from an average of the final five spot indexes at the end of the month in question. This ensures "convergence" between cash and futures—ensures that at the end of the day futures prices are firmly anchored to the "reality" of the physical market and cannot therefore develop an independent life of their own. How to ensure a fair, accurate, dispassionate and independent assessment of what the rate on that particular route was on the settlement date? There was no index and therefore no index panel to make that assessment. So who better than the London Tanker Brokers Panel?

The London Tanker Brokers Panel is a hugely respected London-based committee composed of one representative from EA Gibson, Howard Houlder, Davies and Newman, Clarksons and John I Jacobs (the five largest and most highly respected London tanker brokers) plus two representatives from the Worldscale Organisation. They meet at least once a month mainly to make "awards" to clients who need an expert view of a particular tanker rate. They meet on the first working day after the first of the month, and on that day produce a rate on the route which settles any outstanding contracts. Although at the time of writing this is still an untried settlement method, the degree of respect throughout the oil and the tanker industry for the London Tanker Brokers Panel tends to suggest that it will be a highly acceptable and successful settlement procedure.

At the time of writing (July 1990) so much seems certain, and a BIFFEX committee are working hard on refining the industry's views of which contract will ultimately be feasible. A summary of the latest draft contract will be found on page 78.

The plan seems to be to launch a tanker contract such as this on the BIFFEX Floor within the next six months or so. There certainly seems to be a real industry need for it, and all the initial indications are that it will be a great success.

It is encouraging that BIFFEX and the IPE International Petroleum Exchange are liaising closely on the contract's launch. BIFFEX can supply demonstrable freight futures and shipping expertise; the IPE, of course, is long of oil futures expertise and has achieved a high level of respect within the oil industry. The combination of these talents should be enough to ensure a vibrant and successful contract.

TANKER FREIGHT FUTURES

BIFFEX SHIPPING FUTURES   6 April 1990

Tanker freight:
Crude Oil Contract No. 1

CONTRACT SPECIFICATION

Contract unit:	(a)	1,000 metric tonnes of Crude Oil freight on a voyage on worldscale terms (WS) Arabian Gulf (excluding Iran) to US Gulf, for a tanker of about two hundred and fifty thousand tonnes of oil capacity.
	OR	
	(b)	1,000 metric tonnes of Crude Oil freight on a voyage on Worldscale terms (WS) West Africa to US Gulf for a tanker of about one hundred and thirty thousand tonnes of oil capacity.
Price quotation:		Prices are quoted in US dollars and cents per metric tonne.
Trading months:		[Six] consecutive months in addition to the current month.
Minimum price movement:		One US cent per tonne (tick size $10 per contract).
Maximum daily price movement:		US $1.00 per tonne ($1,000 per contract). Market closes for 15 minutes and on re-opening no further limit that day.
Last trading day:		The 3rd Wednesday of the month or, if not a business day, the next working day.
Settlement:		In cash at the Settlement Price published by the Exchange.
Settlement price:		On the 3rd Wednesday of the month or, if not a business day, the next working day, the London Tanker Brokers Panel will assess the WS rate (in quarter points) for that day for the voyage—(a) or (b) above—and that WS rate will be converted to the then current equivalent rate in US dollars and cents for the voyage on WS terms Offshore Oil Terminal Bonny, West Africa, to Louisiana Offshore Oil Terminal (LOOP), US Gulf—or Ras Tanura, Saudi Arabia, to LOOP which will be the Settlement Price published. The assessment will be given after trading hours.

Note: On the last business day of each week, The Exchange will publish the London Tanker Brokers Panel's assessment at the WS rate for the voyage—(a) or (b) above. The Exchange will publish both the WS rate assessment and the equivalent rate in US dollars and cents for the Settlement Price Voyage, for market information purposes.

CHAPTER 8

OIL FUTURES FOR THE SHIPOWNER

BY SALLY CLUBLEY

Freight rates are, of course, not the only important costs to a shipowner. In addition to the cost of buying or building the vessel and daily running costs are the costs of any particular voyage, in particular port and canal dues and the cost of fuel. Any fluctuation in the oil price, whether upwards or downwards, will affect the per metric tonne voyage rate but will have no effect on the net return to the shipowner. The effect of this fluctuation will reduce the efficiency of the freight futures hedge.

An owner may, for example, have sold freight futures over a forward period as a "blanket hedge" because he feared a drop in freight rates. If he was right, and rates did indeed fall, his BIFFEX hedge will have placed him in a good position as his futures profit will compensate for the losses involved in running his ships. If over the same period, however, bunker prices had increased his hedge would be adversely affected. Although PMT freight rates, and therefore the BFI and BIFFEX futures prices, will have increased more or less in proportion to the change in the oil price, the net return to the owner, after deduction of the bunker price, will be no different. It is more than likely that under these circumstances the owner would be losing money on both his futures hedge and the running of his ships.

A freight futures hedge on its own does not, therefore, provide a sufficient hedge for the shipowner. It is necessary to hedge the bunker fuel price as well as the freight rate to ensure the best available forward cover. Even if an owner decided not to take a freight futures hedge, he might be interested in protecting himself against a change in the bunker fuel price. Such a hedge would also be of interest to a charterer, who will have to pay freight rates which directly reflect the change in the bunker price, and to the bunker industry, both traders and producers.

Bunker hedging works in a very similar way to freight rate hedging, with one major difference. The BIFFEX futures price is an index based on a basket of per metric tonne voyage rates. The oil futures markets, of which there are several, are based on the price of one particular grade of oil in a specified location.

There are three fuel oil contracts traded on futures markets at present, on London's International Petroleum Exchange (IPE), the New York Mercantile Exchange (NYMEX) and the Singapore International Monetary Exchange (SIMEX). The contracts differ in specification details, but are all operated in the same way. None of these contracts enjoys a high level of liquidity as yet, but they are all relatively new and should improve.

As well as the fuel oil contracts, there are others of interest to bunker hedgers, notably the IPE's gas oil contract and the equivalent, called heating oil, on NYMEX. Both NYMEX and the IPE also trade crude oil contracts, which might also be of interest in certain circumstances. Further crude oil contracts are planned on all three exchanges, which should provide still better cover.

When hedging bunker fuel the first step is to establish which of the futures contracts has the closest correlation with the fuel to be hedged. It need not necessarily be the same product, so the hedger need not be deterred by low volumes on the fuel oil markets. Provided that the product being hedged has a close price relationship with the futures contract, a futures hedge will provide satisfactory cover.

The IPE gas oil and fuel oil contracts, the most attractive to bunker hedgers, enable a bunker user or producer to buy or sell oil forward in lots of 100 tonnes. The product specification is detailed by the exchange, as are the delivery details. Both prices are based on the cost of the product in the Amsterdam, Rotterdam, Antwerp area for the specified contract month. The gas oil market is what is known as a physical delivery market. Prices are quoted f.o.b. ARA, and when the contract expires the outstanding unclosed contracts are settled by the physical transfer of gas oil of the IPE specification being delivered in the ARA region.

The fuel oil contract, like the BIFFEX contract, has a cash settlement when the contract expires. In this case, the contracts are settled at the IPE Fuel Oil Index price. This index is published daily and is the mean of cash market assessments of the f.o.b. barge price and c.i.f. cargo price of high sulphur fuel oil in the ARA region. The cash market assessments are based on those published in the various reporting media at the close of business London time.

A straightforward hedge for a ship owner would work in the following way. He would assess the amount of heavy fuel oil and marine diesel he is likely to require over a given time period (the gas oil market trades nine months forward, the heavy fuel oil six months) and hedge any risk of upward price movement he considers unacceptable by buying the equivalent amount of fuel oil and gas oil futures contracts. Then, if prices rise, he will have futures profits to offset against the higher costs of his fuel.

For example, a shipowner might have decided in mid-1989 that he wished to hedge his fuel oil requirement for January 1990 using the IPE fuel oil contract. He would therefore have bought January fuel oil in, say, July 1989 and then, when he purchased his physical supply, closed out his futures position by selling his futures contracts. When he purchases his physical oil, the January futures contract will have become the spot month and will therefore be trading at virtually the same price as the physical market.

		Futures	*Physical*
15 Jul	Bought Jan futures	$80	$86.50
8 Jan	Sold Jan futures	$105	
	Bought physical		$102
	Futures profit	$25	
	Effective buying price		$77

If the fuel oil price had fallen over the time the shipowner had his hedge he would have lost money on the futures contract, but would have bought his physical fuel oil at a lower price. By hedging on the futures market he is locking into the price at which he enters the market, whatever happens to the actual price in the meantime.

BASIS TRADING

Anyone using the oil futures markets has to consider what is known as the "basis". This is the difference between the price of what he is trading and the futures price. The basis will vary according to the differences in specification and location between the product being traded physically and that which is traded on the exchange. It will not always be the same, even for the same product. For example, a shortage of supply in one particular location will not affect prices elsewhere, but will change the basis between that product and the futures price.

Although the basis will vary, it will normally fluctuate less widely than the overall market, so that a hedge is still effective. The exception to this might be if the futures price remains the same over the period of a hedge but the basis varies. But hedges are usually put on by those wishing to protect themselves against a major move in the price, so changes in the basis are not, in most cases, sufficient reason not to hedge.

The basis is quoted using the futures price as the reference point. Thus if the basis is "3 over" it means that the physical price is $3 higher than the futures price, while "2 under" means the cash price is $2 lower than the futures.

It is possible, by using a technique known as basis trading, to move away from the quotation of a fixed price for physical oil. It is one of the means by which supply and pricing of physical oil can be separated.

For example, a trader buys diesel at $145.00 MT and then sells futures as a hedge, at, say, $150.00 MT. He has therefore sold futures $5 above his cash price, or he has a basis of 5 under. In order to make a profit, he must therefore sell the diesel at less than 5 under. He will therefore look for a buyer at, say, 3 under. The price will not be quoted in absolute terms: he will offer the product at 3 under the specified futures price.

By trading in this way, the direction of price movement becomes unimportant; it is the basis which determines profit or loss.

Physicals	*Futures*
Buys gas oil at $145.00 (5 under)	Sells gas oil at $150.00
Sells gas oil at $140.00 (3 under)	Buys gas oil at $143.00
Physical loss of $5.00	Futures profit of $7.00

Net profit of $2.00 MT

If the market had moved up instead of down, the trader would have made a physical profit and a futures loss, but the net profit would have remained at $2.00 MT.

Provided that an acceptable basis risk is present it is possible to hedge a product on a futures market with a very different specification. For example, some bunker hedgers will use the gas oil or crude oil futures markets to hedge on, because of their greater liquidity than fuel oil futures. Provided that the basis risk does not negate the effects of the hedge, this can be a very useful alternative.

SALE ON BUYER'S CALL/TRIGGER PRICING

This technique is a development of basis trading. The two parties to a physical transaction agree all the details of the physical delivery of the oil, but instead of negotiating a fixed price they agree to use the futures price and a differential, or basis.

Returning to the example used above: the seller of the oil was not interested in the price agreed but in the basis. The absolute price would, however, have been important to the buyer. So, having agreed the deal, the two parties might have agreed that the buyer would decide when to price the contract. The seller has already locked in his profit of $2.00 MT whatever the price at which the futures contracts are bought back. So he agrees to let the buyer choose when to buy the futures contracts.

This might be done by allowing the buyer to telephone the seller's futures broker when he wants to price the contracts or, more probably, by the buyer telephoning the seller and saying when he wants to buy. The seller will then buy back his futures contracts, subtract the $3 basis and invoice the seller at the absolute buying price.

Deals such as this would always involve a "fail-safe" clause, enabling the seller to buy back his futures contracts on a specific date if the buyer has not exercised his rights. This date would be agreed between the two and would usually be the final day of a futures contract's life. This ensures that the seller does not still hold a futures position when the contract expires.

The advantage to the buyer is that he has the flexibility to choose when to price the oil and has separated the determination of that price from the physical supply of the oil he needs. He will still have to decide at what moment to buy, but he will not be forced to pay the prevailing price on the day he needs the oil. And the seller has lost nothing by granting this flexibility because his profit was determined by the basis and not by the absolute price.

This technique is increasingly used across the oil industry and is often called trigger pricing, because the buyer decides when to trigger the pricing clause of the physical transaction. Similar deals might be arranged where the seller has the option of choosing when to price, in which case it would be a purchase on seller's call, but this is rather less frequent.

EXCHANGE FOR PHYSICALS

This is another increasingly popular means of separating price from supply of physical oil. Under this type of transaction the two parties exchange their futures positions for physical ones: thus someone who has hedged his bunker requirements by buying futures contracts will give those contracts to his supplier in exchange for the physical oil. Or a supplier who has sold futures as a hedge will give his contracts to his buyer.

As with a trigger pricing deal, buyer and seller agree all aspects of the physical transaction (delivery, product specification, payment terms, etc) but agree to use the futures contracts to determine the price. A date is agreed on which the exchange for physical (e.f.p.) will be registered with the futures exchange.

There are two ways of agreeing an e.f.p. One is usually used for long-term supply deals and one for those involving prompt purchases. Looking first at the long-term deals, a supplier and his customer may have had a long-term relationship with which they are quite happy, but the buyer may think that he would like more price flexibility. He does not, however, wish to jeopardise his supply arrangements. So he might agree to do an e.f.p.

Say the buyer is taking 5,000 tonnes of gas oil each month from his supplier. The physical transfer of the gas oil takes place on the 3rd of the month and the price has normally been determined by the published price quoted on that day. Using an e.f.p. deal the physical details of the contract would remain unchanged, but instead of using the published price, buyer and seller would agree to register an e.f.p. on the IPE on the 3rd of each month and they would each then be free to price whenever they wanted.

The buyer of the physical oil has from any time between agreement to the deal and the expiry of the contract to establish his price by buying futures contracts on the IPE. Similarly the seller can choose his preferred time for selling contracts.

EXCHANGE FOR PHYSICALS

Then on the 3rd of each month (or the nearest business day) the two parties would inform the IPE, through their brokers, that they were registering a 50 lot e.f.p. The physical buyer would sell 50 contracts to the supplier at an agreed price. This price, as will be seen, is irrelevant and will usually be the prevailing market price. This is the only time at which a transaction can be done on the futures market without using open outcry. The market is told merely that the two brokers have registered a 50 lot e.f.p. in the relevant month. The price is not disclosed to the market, though it is to the Exchange. The e.f.p. registration price is then used by the Exchange to close out the positions of both buyer and seller. (If one side has not yet established a position, the e.f.p. will create one.)

The two parties have to agree a differential to the futures price. This is the same as the basis and reflects any quality or locational differences between the product concerned and the futures specification.

When the e.f.p. is registered the seller will invoice the buyer at the e.f.p. price plus or less the discount. Both sides will then add their futures profit or loss to their buying or selling price to obtain their net price.

One month's example can be shown as follows, where a discount of $1.00 from the futures price is agreed.

Buyer:	Futures bought	$87.00	Seller:	Futures sold	$94.00
	e.f.p. registered	$91.00		e.f.p. registered	$91.00
	futures profit	$4.00		futures profit	$3.00
	invoiced at	$90.00		invoices buyer	$90.00
	futures profit	$4.00		futures profit	$3.00
	net price	$86.00		net price	$93.00

Thus it can be seen that the actual registration price of the e.f.p. is irrelevant, because it is also the invoice price. It can also be seen that both buyer and seller fix their price when they enter the futures market. The buyer pays his futures price less the $1.00 discount, while the seller receives his selling price less the $1.00 discount.

In this way both parties to the deal have fixed their own price. Not only is this price different for each party, but it is unknown to the other.

If the physical transaction involves immediate delivery of the oil, one party to the transaction may already have a futures position.

For example, in a similar 5,000 metric tonne transaction the buyer might have hedged his purchase by buying 50 lots of futures. When he arranges physical delivery from the seller, he will arrange an e.f.p., which will be registered in the same way as in the first example, effectively transferring the buyer's 50 lot long position to the seller. The theory is the same, though the effect is slightly different.

This separation of price and supply is increasingly attractive in volatile markets because it enables buyers and sellers to maintain their normal supply or outlet channels while increasing their pricing flexibility.

OVER-THE-COUNTER MARKETS

Over the last two or three years, a large and increasingly complex over-the-counter market has developed in crude oil and oil products. This market is unregulated and is not based in an exchange or any other fixed marketplace but has been created by investment banks to enable participants in the oil markets to lay off risk.

These banks, often known as Wall Street refiners, and others such as the major oil companies who offer the same service provide a series of financial instruments to enable producers, traders or consumers to pass the risk over to someone else at a known cost. Normally, this cost is not in the form of a fee for the service but is built into the price of the instrument offered.

In some cases, these instruments are very similar to, or even the same as, those provided by the futures and options markets, but in most cases they are more specific to the needs of the customer and can be tailored to meet his exact requirements. For example, the futures markets virtually all offer an options contract. A Wall Street refiner will offer those same options contracts, but will also offer options on crudes and products not traded on the futures markets. For example, a bunker user could ask for an option price on bunker fuel for delivery in Hamburg.

Over-the-counter options operate in the same ways as options on futures contracts, except that the transaction is made with a counterparty rather than with the market so it cannot simply be sold back to the market. On the other hand, the Wall Street refiners and major oil companies will give an option designed to suit the customer, adjusting strike prices and expiration periods as well as product details. They can thus be made to fit very closely to a customer's needs.

The other types of instrument offered vary from time to time, and the companies, often known as market-makers, concerned will often be prepared to create a new instrument for a customer, provided they feel there is enough potential. The most commonly-used instruments, apart from options, are probably fixed price sales or purchases over a long period, trigger pricing deals and swaps.

The fixed price purchases and sales are similar to any other purchase or sale on the market. For example, a ship operator may telephone a market-maker and ask for a price for the delivery of 5,000 tonnes per month of bunker C in Piraeus for the next 18 months. The market-maker will quote a price and the buyer will be able to decide whether or not this is attractive to him. If agreed, the price, or prices, will be guaranteed over the specified period, whatever happens to the market. If the buyer later decides, however, that he does not like the price, there is no open market on which to sell his commitment; he will have to go back to the market-maker and negotiate a price to get out of the deal.

Trigger pricing works in the same way as it does when using the futures market. Buyer or seller agrees with the market-maker to buy or sell a specified amount of product to be priced at his option. When he wishes to exercise the pricing option, he simply tells the market-maker. Prices may be triggered for the whole contracted amount or a part of it.

Another major area of the over-the-counter (OTC) market is swaps. A swap deal involves buying or selling at a fixed price now and reversing the transaction at a floating price later. For example, the buyer of 5,000 tonnes per month of bunker fuel in Hamburg might agree to price his requirement over the next 18 months at a specified price for each month. As each month appears, he will sell that commitment back to the Wall Street refiner at a floating price, usually based on a published price over a range of days.

Thus he might agree to buy 5,000 tonnes per month and the price for, say, ten months ahead is $95.00 MT. The deal is to be reversed over the first ten days of the month, using the average price published in one of the price-reporting telexes. This price, for the tenth month, is $100.00 MT. He then sells back his commitment to the market-maker for $100.00 MT and purchases his physical requirements on the market as normal, using the $5.00 profit to reduce the cost of his purchase to $95.00 MT. It therefore operates in the same way as a futures hedge. The main attraction of this kind of deal is that it enables a buyer or seller to lock in a price in an otherwise illiquid market.

These instruments are changing all the time, adapting to prevailing market conditions and the requirements of customers. Their main advantage is that they can be adapted to meet specific requirements, whereas futures markets are designed to be liquid markets trading a standard contract. The main disadvantage is that they are unregulated and there is no open market in the over-the-counter instruments, so an unwanted option or position cannot simply be traded away. It is usually possible to reverse the deal with the original counterpart, but the price may be unattractive. It is also possible to take out a new deal, effectively reversing the first one, with another market-maker, but this can lead to complex administrative procedures when the deals expire.

Over-the-counter deals can also be expensive, particularly for unusual transactions. The market-maker is taking on the unwanted risk and the greater that risk is, the higher will be the price charged. They do, however, offer a further alternative to the use of futures and options.

Using oil futures and options in one of the world's energy futures exchanges and increasingly now using some of the more sophisticated and tailor-made over-the-counter options, the shipping industry—owners, charterers and operators alike—can reduce or remove the unwelcome risks associated with the very volatile world oil price. BIFFEX can help them manage their freight market risk, oil futures and options their bunker market risk. It will come as no surprise to hear that futures and options can also be used to solve the third of their major market-related problems—fluctuations in interest rates and currencies. The next chapter will demonstrate how.

CHAPTER 9

THE SHIPOWNER'S USE OF FINANCIAL FUTURES AND OPTIONS

BY HUGH MORSHEAD

The third primary area of commercial risk faced by a shipowner is that of financial risk. The combination of burgeoning international capital flows, freely floating exchange rates and dismantling of qualitative credit restrictions in the 1980s has noticeably enhanced both currency and interest rate volatility.

In the foreign exchange market, the 1980s were characterised by an "overshoot" in dollar strength up to 1985 followed by its sharp retracement. Such volatility under a fixed exchange rate regime would have been severely restricted. Moreover, interest rates as opposed to credit controls became the fulcrum of monetary policy in the 1980s, with a result that interest rate moves were more frequent and sharper.

The use of financial futures and options gives shipowners and

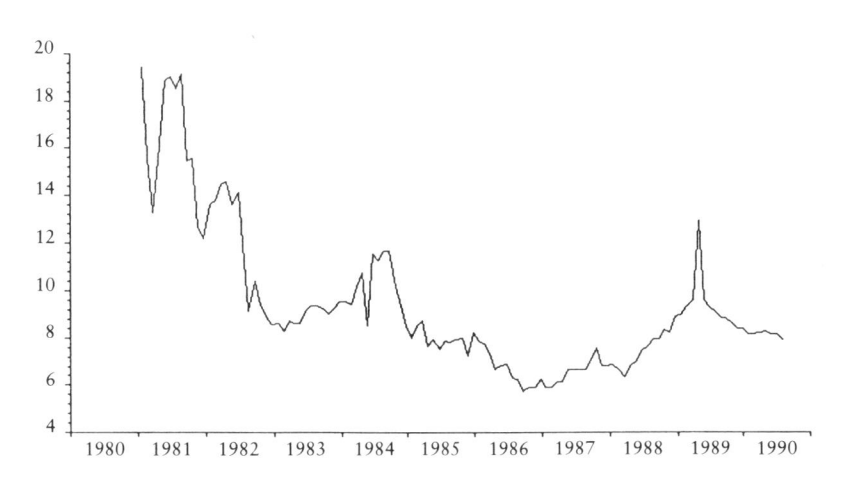

Figure 15. Bank of England US Dollar trade-weighted index

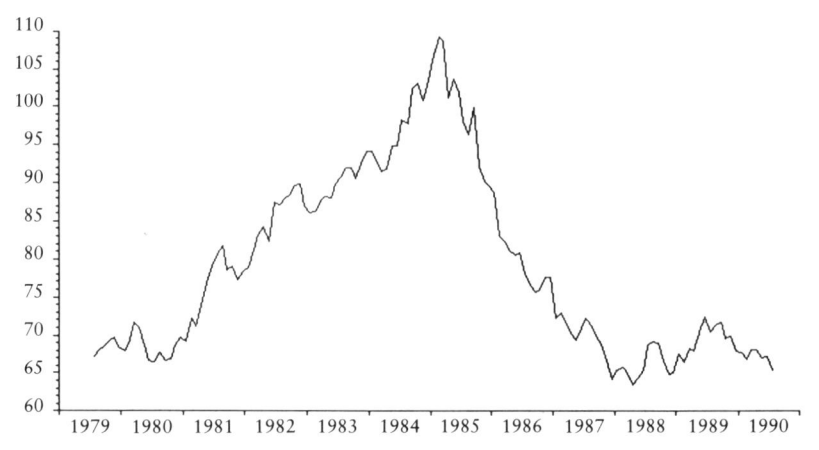

Figure 16. US Federal Funds Rates 1980/90

charterers alike the opportunity of taking protection against changes in the financial status quo.

1. FINANCIAL HEDGING USING FUTURES

Exactly the same principles of hedging can be applied to the financial risks of interest rate and foreign currency fluctuations as to freight market fluctuations.

(a) **Interest rate futures**

At the time of writing there are contracts traded on three-month interest rates of many currencies, the principal ones being US Dollar, Deutschmark, Pound Sterling and French Franc. The price expresses the rate of interest which would be chargeable at the London Interbank Offered Rate (LIBOR) at set dates in the future on set amounts of a notional loan for periods of three months thereafter.

FINANCIAL HEDGING USING FUTURES

The price is always expressed as 100 minus the interest rate.

		Price
Therefore an interest rate of	7% =	93.00
and	8% =	92.00
Therefore an increase of	1% = a fall in futures of	1.00

or 100 basis points

The notional contract sizes of three month interest rate futures are as follows:

			Value of basis point
1. Eurodollars	CME/LIFFE	$1,000,000	$25
2. Euro DM	LIFFE	DM1,000,000	DM25
3. Domestic Sterling	LIFFE	£500,000	£12.50
4. French Franc	MATIF	FF5,000,000	FF125

Example 1

(1) A borrower has $20 million borrowing based on three month LIBOR, which he expects to want to rollover at the next due date and which for the sake of this example is assumed to be the futures delivery date. He has yet to negotiate the loan with the bank, but is worried that rates may shortly rise from 7% to 8%. He therefore regards himself as having an exposure to a rise of interest rates for the three months from the rollover date. Exposure in futures terms equates to 20 lots (i.e., $20m/$1,000,000).

(2) Action: Sell 20 lots Eurodollar futures at 93.00. Suppose market rates indeed rise by 1% by the time the loan rate is fixed at rollover.

(3) Action: Fix loan at currently prevailing rates of 8% and at the same time buy back the futures contract at 92.00.

(4) What is the net cost of the three-month US dollar loan to the borrower?

Loan rate fixed at	8%
Profit on futures sold 93.00	
bought 92.00	1%
Net cost to borrower of three-month loan	7%

(b) Currency futures

Currency futures represent the forward rate of exchange obtainable today for a specified date in the future. The difference between the spot rate and the forward rate is a function of the disparity of interest rates between the two currencies out to the forward date of the futures contract. It is thus possible to trade to a forward date through the anonymity of an exchange as an alternative to covering forward with a bank.

Example 2

(1) A shipowner has US dollar income, but a large part of his expenses are in DM. For the sake of the example it is assumed that the DM expenses are due to be settled at the specified futures date when dollar income will also be available. The shipowner is attracted to today's futures rate of exchange for buying DM and selling dollars. DM expenses are DM1,000,000 (equating to eight lots of futures on Chicago Mercantile Exchange).

(2) Action: Buy eight lots DM futures (60 US cents per DM). Assume that the US dollar weakens against the DM and each DM future will be worth 64 cents.

(3) Alternative strategy A: Take delivery from the exchange at a rate of 64 US cents per DM and offset the futures profit. Alternative strategy B: Purchase DM at 64 US cents per DM in the cash market and sell out the futures purchased at 60. The net result of the action will be:

Currency purchased in cash market at	64 cents/DM
Profit on futures Bought at 60	
Sold at 64	4 cents/DM
Net cost of DM	60 cents/DM

2. FINANCIAL HEDGING USING OPTIONS

Option trading has existed for many years, but has only recently gained popularity for use in conjunction with other financial instruments. The buyer of an option, whether on an exchange or from another principal, has the right to buy or sell one instrument for another at an agreed rate at some specific time in the future.

The trade in options is full of jargon, so it is important not to be deterred by unusual expressions or terms.

(a) The right to buy

The right to buy is called the call option. The buyer of the call option has the right to purchase an agreed quantity of an underlying

FINANCIAL HEDGING USING OPTIONS

security at an agreed price known as the strike price on or before a certain date in the future called the expiry date. The cost of the option is called the option premium and the buyer of an option can lose no more than the option premium he puts up.

Example 3

(1) The shipowner with local DM expenses referred to in Example 2, although attracted by the current rate of 60 US cents per DM, suspects that the exchange rate may go in his favour, i.e., below 60. However, not wanting to take chances he is prepared to take cover for a worst case exchange rate of US cents 62 for DM for a premium of US 0.26 cents per DM.

(2) Action: Buy eight lots of DM 62 calls for a premium of US cents 0.25 per DM.

The cost to the shipowner is never any greater than the option premium paid, i.e., US cents 0.25 per DM. The reason for this is that the holder of the option will only exercise his right to buy DM if the spot exchange rate is above the strike price. If the spot is below the strike price then the holder of the option will ignore his right to buy above the current market and will

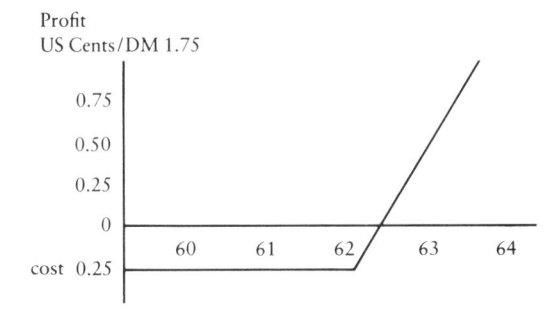

Figure 17.   Graph of DM 62 call option at expiry

purchase the underlying currency at the more favourable prevailing cash market rate. The only cost to him will have been the option premium.

(3) The market moves to DM 64 at expiry which is the time when the local DM expenses are due to be paid. What is the effective exchange rate for the shipowner?

Strike price of option	62.00
Option premium	0.25
Net exchange rate	62.25 US cents per DM

(4) In this instance the call option was used as cover for a worst case. Further study will show that it is possible to take advantage of a best case exchange rate using options by the granting or selling of put options, the purchase of which is considered below.

(b) The right to sell

The right to sell is called the put option. The buyer of a put option has the right to sell an agreed quantity of an underlying security at a strike price on or before a certain expiry date for a given option premium.

Example 4

In Example 1 we saw how the borrower of $20 million who had yet to determine the interest rate on a rollover loan, fixed his rate in the futures market at a price of 7% or 93.00 in futures terms.

(1) An alternative would have been to purchase a put option with a strike price of say, 92.50, i.e., 7.5%, if there was less certainty about the movement in rates. Let us say that the cost of this would be 0.10. Remember that the price of 92.50 equates to a three-month interest rate of 7.5%, considered to be the worst case possibility.

(2) However, on this occasion let us assume that the interest rate did not rise but remained 7%.

What would have been the result?

Since interest rate did not reach 7.5% the buyer of the put option would not have exercised his option. Instead he rolled over his loan at 7% and the option premium paid of 0.10% equated to an additional cost. The all-in cost to the borrower therefore would have been 7.10%.

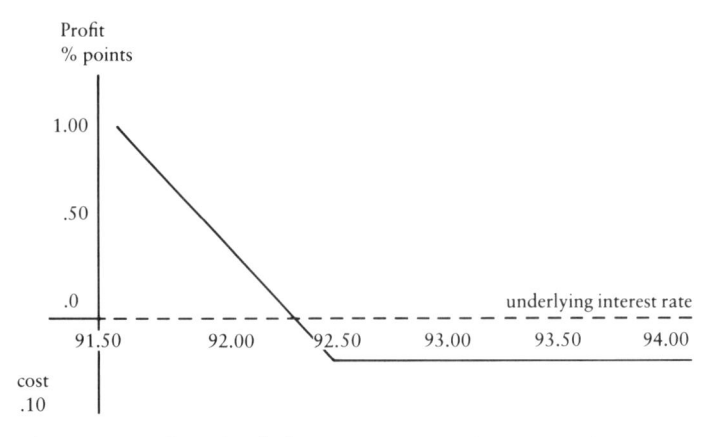

Figure 18.   *Graph of the 92.50 put option at expiry*

CONCLUSION 95

This is the reverse shape to that of the call option discussed in Example 3, and proves that his particular position comes into profit at 92.50 less 0.10, i.e., 92.40.

Some extra notes on options

(1) Options with the right of exercise at any time until expiry are said to be US style. Options which give the right of exercise on expiry day only are known as European style.

(2) An option which is profitable at expiry is said to be "in the money", whereas one which is not is said to be "out of money". The option whose strike price is at the same level as the underlying spot is said to be "at the money".

(3) The premium on options which are out of the money and at the money represent the value placed on the time left until expiry. This is to reflect the risk taken by the seller or grantor that the options will be exercised at or before expiry.

(4) An option will only be exercised if it is in the money at expiry. Until that time, the value of an in-the-money option will be represented by two components:

(i) Intrinsic value—the extent that the option is in the money.
(ii) Time value—the option price less intrinsic value.

(5) The price of an option will be offered taking into account a variety of factors which will include:

— a view of the volatility of the underlying security.
— the time left until expiry of the option.
— the level of the strike price compared to the spot.

(6) Options are ideally used for both balance sheet and trading income exposures alike.

3. CONCLUSION

Space has allowed us really only to touch on the wide-ranging and fast-developing world of financial futures and options, and how these sophisticated financial instruments can help the shipowner and his treasurer. A schedule of some of the contracts offered on the

London International Financial Futures Exchange and other contracts around the world is given in Appendix VII.

There can, however, be no reasonable doubt that the new breed of risk-conscious shipowner will make financial hedging a major weapon in his arsenal. The control of the risks of adverse currency and interest rate fluctuations, like the control of market and bunker price risk, must become second nature to the successful shipowner of the new generation.

CHAPTER 10

THE PRACTICALITIES OF FUTURES TRADING

To the uninitiated outside observer, the futures markets may seem at first sight arcane, peculiar, even disturbing places. They have a reputation as highly speculative, fortune-creating (or bankrupting) high-rolling casinos. Futures Traders are said to be either burnt-out or millionaires by the age of 30. (At 35 I am glad not to be the former and becoming accustomed to not being the latter). The commonest view of the futures markets (also the most biased and least accurate) is based on a series of newsworthy scandals from the last twenty years: The Bunker Hunt brothers trying to "squeeze" the silver market, "Churn 'em and burn 'em" salesmen taking old ladies to the cleaners, swindling practices in the Chicago pits, manipulations of world commodity prices for the benefit of a few cowboys, the sort of thing graphically illustrated in the feature films "Trading Places" and "Limit Up".

News of large movements in interest rates, or the oil price, or soyabean meal price is accompanied on the television news by library footage of massive hoards of teenagers in coloured jackets yelling and screaming at each other, grimacing in concentration and waving their arms about in apparent mimicry of the tick-tack man at the racecourse. That the crude oil price has soared because of muddled Middle Eastern machinations is not hard to grasp, but what those fellows in the stripey jackets were up to is anyone's guess. Anyhow, time for our late-night Ovaltine....

And much of this is an image which the futures industry itself perpetuates and embellishes. It *is* a fast-moving, exciting, highly-geared business, run at least formerly by a group of wide boys, spivs, hoodlums and hooligans. And a very good job they made of it too.

Fairly recent changes in the regulatory regimes of the world (in the UK, for example, the creation of the industry's own self-regulatory organisation, the Association of Futures Brokers and Dealers or AFBD) have been highly successful in removing those abuses which it is only reasonable to admit did indeed exist in the Futures Industry until five years or so ago. There were indeed swindles, and it is pointless to deny it. But most observers are now quite satisfied that the passing of the Financial Services Act in the UK in 1986 and of similar legislation in the US and elsewhere has been more than sufficient to "clean up the industry". Some old-time commodity brokers and traders would say that it is now too clean, and there have certainly been a fair number of casualties among companies who were either too corrupt to be able to clean up their act sufficiently or for whom the cost of complying with the stringent terms of the Financial Services Act were too great compared to fairly meagre commission income.

Indeed, I tend to the school of thought which says that the City of London made a great mistake in pressing for self-regulation, as opposed to regulation from Whitehall. For this has meant both that we, the practitioners, have had to pay the massive cost of regulation, which otherwise would have been borne by the taxpayer, and also that the poachers whom we have turned into gamekeepers know the game so well that they have perhaps over-regulated, in some instances making it difficult to earn an honest penny. Civil Servants would inevitably have been more inept, the regulations less stringent, and the City more left to its traditional form of "my word my bond" self-regulation. It is probably also true to say that whereas the Financial Services Act set out to protect the private investor from the unscrupulous futures broker, some part of the legislation affects all users of the futures markets. The net may be spread a little too wide. But I have not only strayed from the main thrust of my argument but, as one whose boss is the Chairman of the Association of Futures Brokers and Dealers, may also be sailing rather close to the wind.

The point at any rate is that the traditional image of the futures markets is by and large an unfair and unjustified one, at least in the aftermath of the Financial Services Act. Of course they are exciting and fast-moving markets, but they are now more than sufficiently regulated to ensure their orderliness and security. What's more, they are a great deal more straightforward, simple and easy-to-use than a casual acquaintance might suggest and than some futures brokers (who like to maintain a certain mystique) would like to admit. This chapter therefore aims to explain in straightforward terms how the uninitiated shipping man can set about using the futures markets.

From the point of view of the client, the end-user, the practical considerations are best discussed in three sections:

(1) The relationship with the futures broker (choosing a broker, opening an account, placing orders, the ongoing relationship).
(2) How to trade (the prices, how they move and why, how to monitor them; Trading Disciplines; Monitoring positions and accounting for profits and losses).
(3) Financial considerations.

This chapter will look at each of these aspects in turn.

1. THE RELATIONSHIP WITH THE FUTURES BROKER

For regulatory and practical reasons, all trading on all of the world's regulated exchange-traded futures markets is conducted via authorised, regulated and professional futures broking companies. The exceptions to this rule are the so-called over-the-counter markets trading futures, options or other more sophisticated derivatives in, for example, specialist oil products. These OTC markets (including the international spot and forward foreign exchange market) are principle-to-principle, are not traded on an exchange and are to some degree unregulated. But we are concerned here only with fully regulated exchange-traded futures contracts, such as oil on the IPE and NYMEX, BIFFEX and LIFFE. All trading must be conducted by and through futures brokers who in the UK will be authorised by the AFBD or the Securities and Investments Board.

Futures brokers come in a fairly wide variety of shapes and sizes. Many large users of the various markets—for example, banks, major oil companies and the large grain traders—themselves become members of the various markets, of the AFBD and of the International Commodities Clearing House, and then trade on their own behalf (and occasionally on behalf of clients). Similarly there are many trade houses whose original speciality was in a particular commodity, but who with time have become futures brokers in their own right. Czarnikow and ED & F Man in the London Sugar Terminal Market are examples of this kind of thing. Then there are the UK and American Commission Houses (often known as Futures Commission Merchants or FCMs). These are companies who specialise in trading futures on behalf of clients. Their primary or sometimes sole source of income comes—as the name would suggest—from commission earned from clients. GNI is the largest and most successful UK commission house; Shearson Lehman, Merrill Lynch, Dean Witter and Refco are the giant American FCMs.

Then there is a wide variety of smaller broker/traders who execute business for clients, probably also trade on their own account, perhaps get involved in physical trading, or a wide variety of other futures—or commodity-related businesses. These will very often be privately-owned or small partnerships.

In the American markets in particular there are two groups of people whom you do not normally find in the UK: the "independent" floor broker and the "clearer". The independent is not a member of the clearing house and specialises in actually executing orders in the pits of the massive US exchanges. He will conduct business for outside clients, but have to "give it up" to a nominated clearer. The "clearers" are huge bank-like institutions, who may or may not be represented on the floor of the various exchanges but who make their commission by using their large balance sheets to clear virtually unlimited futures positions.

Smallest—at least in size terms—are the "locals". These are private individuals, often former employees of a futures broker, who make their living in the futures pit usually trading entirely on their own behalf, often buying and selling for a "one tick" profit. These are the people whose speculative activities are really responsible for giving the large exchanges their impressive liquidity. Rules vary from exchange to exchange about how much "locals" are allowed to do, but by and large they are not permitted to trade for outside customers, but may execute orders on behalf of a Futures Commission Merchant who does not happen to have a broker in the particular pit in question.

In practical terms in the UK your choice is among the perhaps 50 medium-to-large commission houses and trade houses who man the London and International Markets, who are members of ICCH and AFBD and whose size, integrity and reputation ensure that your interests in the market are reasonably safeguarded. How do you choose among them?

It might at first be thought that there is a great deal less to choose between futures brokers than there is between, for example, shipbrokers. For unlike the shipping market, the futures markets are entirely open and transparent (i.e., the price paid and the size of the deal, although never the identity of the client, are instantly known worldwide). There can be no such thing as a private and confidential deal. The job which the broker will do for you in terms of actually placing the business therefore might in general terms be thought to be little better nor little worse than the job any other broker might do (although we will below highlight how some brokers will actually trade better on your behalf on the markets than others). So what should you look out for when choosing your broker?

(1) Probity, integrity, reputation and financial standing

The broker is your link to the market, and he will be handling substantial sums of your money. It is obviously therefore vital to make sure that the broking company is of sufficient size, backing and integrity for you to have no worries whatsoever. So ask who owns the company, what its capitalisation is, how many markets it is a member of, is it a member of the Association of Futures Brokers and Dealers, does it segregate clients' funds from its own if requested, does it pay interest on client funds and so on. It is also worth asking whether the broking company trades for its own account (in which case there might occasionally be a conflict of interests), and whether the individual brokers have a personal financial interest in commissions earned from clients (i.e., are they salaried or on a commission?. If the latter there is a risk of "churning" — encouraging excessive trading to generate commission.)

(2) A proven track record of service to clients

Ask about the broker's financial and accounting systems. Are they manual or computerised? How often will you receive account statements and contracts notes? Ask about their market information systems. Will they telephone you on a regular basis with market news? Will you receive regular market reports? Will you be allocated a personal account executive? Ask about their back-up and support services. Can the account be held in any currency? Can it be held off-shore? Do the brokers have a research department? Do they have access to physical spot market information?

(3) A proven trading record

Ask whether they are manning their own seat on the particular market you are interested in. (Although many perfectly respectable futures brokers will actually be trading via other brokers' floor traders, or using self-employed "locals".) Ask about their market share (a low market share may indicate a gap in some of their services). Ask about their client spread.

A detailed discussion along these lines should enable you to choose the broker who comes closest to your particular requirements. If you are likely to be a large volume trader, you may decide to appoint more than one broker. This should increase the service you receive and will prevent any one broker becoming identified particularly with your business. However, the wider you spread your business, the less likely you are to receive a first-class service from any one broker. Choosing the right broker is perhaps one of the most important elements in successful futures trading and is worthy of a good deal of research.

Having chosen a broker, it is worth being aware of some of the historic swindles which can and have occurred in the markets. For while it is true that the UK and US markets have gone through a regulatory revolution in the last few years, which has greatly improved the standing of the markets, and while room for abuse by unscrupulous futures brokers has been hugely narrowed as a result, thus squeezing out the vast majority of the "cowboys", it may be worth outlining some of the ways that historically a futures broker could—if that way inclined—make a dishonest penny out of trading for you. An awareness on your part of the sort of thing which could theoretically happen to your orders is the first step towards spotting abuses. The main swindles which could in the old days have been perpetrated in the futures markets could be summarised as follows:

(a) "Front-running"

The broker, knowing that you have a large order which will probably move the market, trades on his own account ahead of your order, often then selling his own position back to you towards the end of your buying order. The front-runner has clearly no incentive to work hard to achieve the best possible price on the market.

(b) "Clipping"

If you place an order to buy 100 lots of April crude oil futures at US$19.00, it may be that the broker will actually be able to trade at US$18.90. If dishonest, he will take the 100 lots at US$18.90 into his own book and sell them back to you at US$19.00. If he is even cleverer, he will sell them back to you at US$18.95—theoretically you are both happy, but he is still stealing 5 cents from you.

(c) "Crossing"

If it is perfectly obvious, for example, that the market is going down but you give the broker a buy order, he could theoretically "cross" the trade on the market, taking the short side himself. He would of course have been better to advise you to delay your order until the market had moved further in your favour.

(d) "Churning"

Encouraging excessive trading merely to generate increased brokerage, or personal commissions.

These, and a variety of more sophisticated variations on the theme, are some of the ways that a futures broker could historically have swindled you. And it is pointless to try to pretend that this sort of thing has not historically occurred. However, the industry has now sufficiently tightened up on trading practices to ensure that these abuses are exceedingly hard to perpetrate, and very easy to catch.

Nonetheless it is important to be aware of them when choosing a broker. Beware, in particular, of exceedingly low commission rates. In recent years there has been a commission war of increasing severity in most of the world's futures exchanges. And it is right that free competition among futures brokers should lead to the cheapest reasonable way of transacting business for the client. But some brokers will offer ludicrously low commissions. You can be sure that their overheads are as high or higher than the rest, and that if their commissions are that low, that they will be making their money elsewhere.

In general it is probably prudent to be ready to pay a fair market commission to the broker, probably midway between the lowest and highest, and to expect excellence of service, and in particular excellence of executions on the market in return. Above all beware of the short-sighted tendency to screw every last cent out of your broker—you will pay for it in reduced service or poor executions. The honest broker deserves his wage.

So having considered all of these things and landed up with one or at most two futures brokers offering you good coverage of the main markets you are likely to want to use, what happens next? The first, and in some respects most crucial, stage is the agreeing terms with your chosen broker. For most aspects of the client/futures broker relationship are negotiable. It is important therefore to arrive at a clear and fair agreement with the broker in advance of trading. Lack of a clear understanding on both sides of the detail of the agreement between you will ultimately be disastrous.

The main elements you need to agree are: Commission levels (including whether there are special rates for spreads or day-trades); deposit levels (Clearing House Minimum or more); financing arrangements (how do margin calls operate, what happens if they are not met immediately, is there a credit arrangement and so on). The broker will ask you to sign a more-or-less fearsome-looking "Terms of Business letter" or similar account-opening papers. Included in this document will be the full terms and conditions of the relationship between you, a "risk disclosure statement" which clearly states the high risk of trading in any futures market (often to the extent of rather exaggerating those risks), a commission statement, and a statement of "Standard Terms and Conditions of Business". The finer print will rarely be negotiable.

Technically speaking you may trade under UK law as soon as account opening papers have been dispatched to you (so long as you are a "business investor"). But commercial prudence will normally dictate that the broker will require completion and signing, as well as a suitable remittance, before any trading can take place. The terms and conditions under which a futures trading account are opened are always very stringent, mainly because the broker, it will be remembered, is actually acting as a principal on the market, albeit on your behalf as a client. Most brokers therefore adopt a fairly conservative belt-and-braces approach to safeguarding themselves against default by any of their clients. This approach applies both in regulatory and in financial terms. For example, all brokers reserve the right to close your futures positions out at their discretion and without notice (albeit in an orderly manner) if you fail to meet your margin obligations.

Having completed the necessary paperwork and familiarised yourself with your chosen broker's standard operating procedures, you will be required by the broker to make a suitable "account opening deposit" with him prior to trading. This will take the form most often of a cash deposit, or in some cases and on some markets (but not the US markets) a credit arrangement. How much you deposit with the broker is largely negotiable and is a function of how much you intend to trade. Few brokers will open a private trading account for less than about $25,000 or so, and if you are a hedging client, you will probably be thinking in terms of hundreds of thousands rather than tens of thousands. (Exact financial considerations will be explained a little later.)

The broker will hold this money for you and will use it against deposits, variations margins and commissions, always of course, accounting for it in full. At your instruction he will hold your funds in either a "segregated" or "non-segregated" account. A "segregated" account is an account which is entirely separate from the broker's own funds, and which would be inviolate and untouchable by other creditors in the event of the broker's bankruptcy. All inexperienced private client accounts in the UK now have—by law—to be "segregated". But accounts for experienced private clients, business investors and professional investors (i.e., other futures brokers') may be non-segregated, and therefore theoretically at risk in the event of the broker becoming bankrupt.

Which should you opt for? Clearly, if you are in any doubt at all about the good standing of the broker, you should insist on a segregated account to give you complete security. But arguably if you have doubts about the standing of the broker, you should not have been using them in the first place. And the futures broker will probably offer less attractive terms for segregated accounts than for non-segregated. For example, he will not allow trading on a credit line to any segregated account, and it is likely that deposits and commissions will be higher. What's more, many futures brokers will be reluctant to offer businesses segregated accounts, reserving them for small private clients. The reason for this is that the broker can offset one client's positions against another's in the clearing house if they are non-segregated. This means that the broker will be "net margined" — i.e., the broker's obligations for non-segregated accounts will be offset by the clearing house obligations to the broker. The end result will often be a fairly low cash-flow between the broker and the clearing house so far as non-segregated accounts are concerned. Segregated accounts have to be margined at the Clearing House in full, thereby involving a cash-flow consideration for the broker.

So there may well be advantages for the client in opting for a non-segregated account, despite the apparent higher security risk than a segregated one. And if the broker is of a sufficient size, backing, integrity and repute, there should really be very little risk inherent in maintaining a non-segregated account with him.

At last we have reached the stage where you have selected your broker, signed his account opening papers and agreed full terms with him, opened an account and lodged sufficient funds in it to cover your anticipated trading.

So how does the trading actually occur? Compared to the complexities of planning your hedge, choosing a broker and opening an account with him, the actual trading is extremely straightforward. The planning of your hedge, to use BIFFEX as an example, should result in a list of requirements along the following lines:

"Buy 50 lots nearby April at 1500 or better."
"Buy 50 lots nearby July at 1300 or better."
"Buy 50 lots nearby October at 1400 or better."

You should bear in mind a few points about placing orders with your broker, the most important of which is complete clarity. Since most trading will be conducted on the phone, there is plenty of room for errors, so it is vitally important to be absolutely clear that he understands precisely what it is that you want him to do. If you yourself make a slip, and inadvertently say "buy" when you meant

RELATIONSHIP WITH FUTURES BROKER

to say "sell", you will find most likely that the broker, who tape-records all telephone conversations, will ask you to bear the cost of the error. So it is always worth repeating orders back and forth to one another at least a couple of times. Always use the same format to place an order. The above suggestion is acceptable, although most futures brokers will use the forms:

"Pay 1500 or less for 50 lots (half a hundred) nearby April."
"Sell 50 lots nearby June at 1300."

thereby clearly differentiating between a buy order and a sell order. Whatever format you use the important thing is that both your broker and you should be absolutely clear about what it is you are trying to achieve.

Keep a careful note in some kind of trading book or form of exactly what it is that you have asked the broker to do. And keep an accurate note of the precise timings of every aspect of the transaction. This helps you to monitor trading. The following is an example of what a completed trading form might look like:

Date:

			Order				Execution		
REF	BROKER	TIME ORDER PLACED	QUANTITY	MONTH	MARKET	PRICE	QUANTITY	PRICE	TIME
1	GNI	1115	+50	April '90	BIF	Mkt	+10	1495	1120
							+20	1496	1122
							+20	1496	1125
2	GNI	1126	+50	July '90	BIF	1300	+25	1294	1134
							+15	1298	1140
		1140	increased authority to "market"				+10	1304	1141
3	GNI	1543	+50	Oct '90	BIF	1400	+30	1399	1550
							+20	1400	1552

Figure 19. Completed trading form

Such a form is essential to keep track of your trading, to keep your administration department up to date with what you are doing, and to check the recaps and contract notes which you will be receiving from the broker after trading.

Actual trading is conducted quite simply on the telephone with your broker. Any other form of communication (telex, fax) is likely to be too slow and cumbersome, although you may wish to reconfirm telephone orders using telex or fax. You will normally trade with an "account executive" in the brokers' office, although if you are a large trade client the broker may sometimes give you access direct to the floor of the exchange. However, beware of demanding access to the floor too lightly. You will find that the floor trader or booth broker is unwilling to talk on the phone more than is absolutely necessary for him to get your order down. He will probably give you a slightly better feel of the market than the desk dealer can, but you may well be sacrificing other aspects of the service. And although many clients tell themselves that they need access to the floor for speed of execution, it is probably comparatively rarely that split-second timing is necessary. (You may also sometimes be quicker going via the office anyhow—there must be a limit to the number of phones the floor can answer at any one moment, and a squawk-box link between office and floor gives you virtually instantaneous access to the market via the broker's office.)

The broker will recap your trading by telex at the end of the day and should send you a contract note and account statement the following morning by post or by electronic mail. It is important to check both of these confirmations against your own trading record. Errors do occur, and the important principle is spotting them as soon as possible, trading out of the error "at market" whatever the cost may be. By that means you quantify the cost of the error, and prevent the market from moving any further against you. Spotting errors, facing up to them and trading out of them at market is the first of many trading disciplines you will have to apply if you are to have a happy and successful futures trading experience. It is trading disciplines such as this which form the main part of the next section: How to trade.

Before moving on to that, a word about your continuing relationship with your futures broker. Futures broking is heavily dependent on personal relationships. You will quickly develop a close rapport with your account executive. And arguably the closer you can get to him the better it will be. In a sense, you and the broker are partners in a war against the markets. It is important that you should both know exactly what the other means, and that you should be certain that you are both fighting the same war.

In particular, you should with time be able to build up a high degree of trust in your broker, you should be happy to reveal more and more of your trading strategy to him, take him more and more into your confidence. Whereas, for example, you may be reluctant to begin with to tell even your broker the full size of your planned trading programme, you should become increasingly confident in doing so. If for example you have a very large buying order in mind, perhaps large enough potentially to move the market, you will be better off discussing confidentially with the broker how best to place the business. Never feed him little bits at a time, as his approach to the market will probably be very different depending on the size of the ultimate buying programme. Do not broker your broker. He is better at it than you ever can be. So a proper broker/client relationship will become closer and closer with time, the client revealing more and more about his trading to his broker. The broker will always respect the client's confidences; he has no reason not to, and a broken confidence will speedily result in a lost client.

Assuming, then, a good close relationship with your broker, let us move on to the meat: how to trade?

2. HOW TO TRADE ON A FUTURES MARKET

(1) Futures prices

The prices on all futures markets are arrived at by a process of free and open negotiation between a willing buyer and a willing seller. If there are more buyers than sellers, the price will rise until it reaches an equilibrium, and vice-versa. So the prices are effectively a function of the aggregate of views of all of those trading on the market. This means that they are extremely sensitive to any piece of news released about the market. Very often, the prices will appear to be over-sensitive, swinging dramatically one way or another before being corrected. All futures prices are likely to be more volatile (sometimes very much more volatile) than the underlying commodity price. It is this volatility which can offer some worthwhile hedging as well as speculative opportunities.

This volatility of price means that the successful trader (whether hedger or speculator) will need to keep closely in touch with market movements. They will normally do this via their futures broker, although the more active traders may well invest in one of the "real-time" price reporting screens. These screens chronicle the market movements second by second. They usually report the latest bids and offers, the last trade, the high price for the day, the low price for the day, the previous night's closing price and the volume of trade so far today, for example. A typical BIFFEX screen might look something like this:

1	2	3	4	5	6	7	8
	Sell	Buy	Trade	High	Low	Close	Vol
F	911	910	910	910	905	910	107
G	920	919	919	920	911	911	329
J	974	971	971	971	970	971	243
N	843	840	840	840	838	840	4
V	938	935	935	935	932	935	127
F	948	937	937	937	937	937	86
J	1020	1020	1020	1020	1020	1020	30
N	870	860	860	860	860	860	20
V	980	975	975	975	975	975	20

BIFFEX TOTAL = 986
BFI = 1495

Working across the screen from left to right, these columns of figures are:

> (1) The contract month
> (2) Sell: The best price at which any broker is currently offering.
> (3) Buy: The best price at which any broker is bidding. The difference between the buy and sell price is known as the bid/offer spread.
> (4) Trade: The last traded price.
> (5) High: The high price traded today.
> (6) Low: The low price traded today.
> (7) Close: Last night's closing price. Also the price which will have been used to calculate margin requirements.
> (8) Vol: The number of lots traded in that contract today.

Instead of writing the contract months out in full, the screens use the International Stock Exchange mnemonics. These may seem confusing, but will become familiar to the user with time. The mnemonic for January is F (the *f*irst month of the year), the other months following alphabetically, but omitting those letters which might be confused with numbers, so:

> Jan = F   Jul = N
> Feb = G   Aug = Q
> Mar = H   Sep = U
> Apr = J   Oct = V
> May = K   Nov = X
> Jun = M   Dec = Z

HOW TO TRADE

The close and careful monitoring of prices, of major market moves, and of the forces, pressures and news which will move the market is an essential prerequisite of successful use of the market. Apart from the market prices themselves, there are two main forms of analysis which you will find useful: *fundamental analysis*, which is a study of the real influences of supply and demand driving the market one way or the other; and *technical analysis*, the study, using charts, of the way in which the market price has been moving. Technical analysis will be explained and discussed more fully in Chapter 11 "How to Make Money out of Futures". Your broker will be your main source of information about the market. As a norm, if you are a fairly active trade hedger you should expect to receive a routine call from your broker most days. Thereafter it is reasonable for him to expect you to call in if you want to know what is going on. And the broker should be supplying you with reasonably regular market reports and other information. So the first discipline is close and careful monitoring of the market. What are the other trading disciplines?

(2) Trading disciplines

We have already mentioned two or three trading disciplines:

- Keep closely in touch with market movements—never lose track of what is going on in the market, particularly while you have an open position.
- Be absolutely clear in your instructions to your broker and make sure he completely understands what you are trying to do.
- Monitor your trading and your positions yourself and keep a careful record of what you have done (and why), and check recaps and contract notes with some care.
- Face up to errors immediately, trade out of them at market to quantify the cost of the error, and then, and only then, discuss whose error it was, and therefore who should "wear it".
- Be absolutely clear in your own mind why you are trading (hedging or speculating?) and allocate futures profits and losses accurately to a particular piece of business or profit centre.

- Take your broker as much into your confidence as you can. He can only take best advantage of market conditions if he knows exactly what you are trying to achieve, particularly the overall volume you are going to want to trade.

A number of other basic trading disciplines will help you avoid some of the worst pitfalls of futures trading:

- "If in doubt, stay out."
- Never trade for the sake of it. If you don't have a strong view one way or another, don't trade.
- Never buck the trend. ("The trend is your friend".)
- Never believe that you are cleverer than the market unless you are absolutely certain that you have good reason to do so. In particular, if a position is moving against you, be ready to admit loud and clear both to yourself and to others that you were wrong in getting into the position, and that you should now get out of it. A good stop-loss discipline is the best way to do this, particularly if the position is purely speculative ("Stops" will be explained and discussed in full in chapter 11 "Making money with futures")
- Always maintain plenty of liquidity (i.e., spare cash) to finance positions which may be temporarily moving against you. There is nothing worse than being "stopped out at the bottom" for want of funds to pay margin calls.
- Do not try to pick tops or bottoms of a trend. This is effectively bucking the trend, and rarely works. Buy into a rising market, and sell into a falling one is generally good advice, at least in a fully liquid market. In a less liquid market it may sometimes be necessary to buy weakness and sell strength in order to be sure of achieving the kind of volume you are looking for.

These and other similar trading disciplines which you will develop for yourself are essential prerequisites for a successful and happy futures trading experience. Lack of clarity about what you are trying to achieve and the best way to do so is a certain recipe for disaster.

3. WHAT DOES IT COST?

It would clearly be impractical and unattractive if the hedger had to pay the full value of the contracts he is buying or selling on the futures market. An outlay of $1,000,000 for every $1,000,000 of futures cover would have serious cash-flow implications. So to make the futures markets cheap, easy and attractive to use, a system of deposits (the margin system) has been devised over the years. An understanding of the margins system requires an understanding of the clearing house system.

The clearing house system

Unlike a shipbroker who acts as an intermediary between two clients—a shipowner and a charterer—and has no responsibility as a principal for the agreement reached, the futures broker acts as a principal on the market. He will nearly always be acting for a client, executing his orders, but he is nonetheless considered by the market to be acting on his own behalf as a principal.

So when broker A buys a particular contract from broker B on a futures market, the contract is between A and B, despite the fact that A is acting on behalf of client X, and B is acting on behalf of client Y. Moreover, although A has bought the contract from B, it is very likely that when he wants to sell it again, B may well not wish to buy it back. So to maintain the flexibility of the market, the relationship between A and B is severed as soon as the transaction has been registered, and the International Commodities Clearing House (ICCH) in the UK, or similar clearing institutions in overseas markets, steps in as the other half of both deals. So now A has bought from the ICCH, and B has sold to the ICCH. When the time comes for A to sell the contract back to the market, he may well agree a price with C, but again the ICCH steps in between them. The system is perhaps best demonstrated by a diagram, see figure 20, p. 114.

Such a system as this is clearly necessary to allow the complete flexibility of being able to buy or sell on the market at any time. It also effectively guarantees the market. The ICCH is a limited company owned by the UK clearing banks. It guarantees all of the trades done on the UK markets apart from the GAFTA wheat and barley contracts and LTOM—the London Traded Options

114   PRACTICALITIES OF FUTURES TRADING

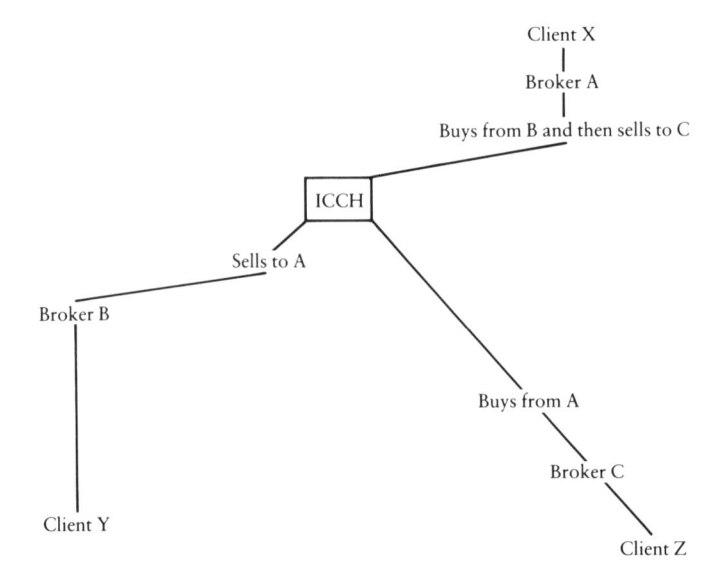

```
                                Client X
                                   |
                                Broker A
                                   |
                        Buys from B and then sells to C
                                  /
                            [ ICCH ]
                   Sells to A /
           Broker B
              |
              |                      Buys from A
              |                            \
              |                          Broker C
              |                              \
           Client Y                         Client Z
```

Figure 20. The clearing house system

Market. Thus if broker A has sold to broker B who then goes bankrupt, broker A's position is nonetheless safeguarded by the ICCH. It is clearly therefore in the interests of the ICCH to try to ensure the good standing of all its member brokers. It does this in a variety of ways.

(1) By making stringent financial requirements of its members.
(2) By requiring the Protected Payments System, under which they have direct access to the broker's funds.
(3) By requiring the brokers to pay a good-faith deposit on each lot bought or sold. This deposit is set by the ICCH at a level which they expect to be sufficient to cover any possible adverse movement in the market, so they can increase the level of the deposit at short notice if they foresee a possibility of the market increasing in volatility. At the time of writing this "Clearing House Minimum Deposit" is set at US$300 per lot for BIFFEX, US$1,000 per lot for London Crude oil.

(4) By requiring the brokers to pay by 10 a.m. every day the amount of money by which the market has moved against any open position they are holding (the "variation" or "maintenance" margin).

So the clearing house system provides the flexibility which the market needs; it guarantees the deals between the brokers; and it applies certain necessary financial disciplines on its clients—the brokers.

The broker-client relationship

Since the futures broker is effectively acting on the market as a principal, and since the ICCH imposes these disciplines, all reputable brokers will pass them on to the client. (If they do not do so, they will have a risk exposure themselves, which, of course, reduces their probity and reliability for other clients.) This means that their clients:

(1) Have to demonstrate their good standing and credit worthiness. (Otherwise the broker should decline to act for them.)
(2) Have to pay a good-faith deposit usually in advance of trading. The level of this deposit is negotiable between the broker and his client and will vary considerably depending on the standing of the client. However, it will very often be at least double the Clearing House Minimum. A double deposit gives the broker the security which he needs.
(3) Have to pay variation margins (the amount by which the market has moved against them) on a daily basis; and
(4) Have to pay the broker an agreed commission.

So what are the main financial considerations in practical terms?

(1) Before trading the broker will require the client to lodge an account-opening deposit with him. This sum is negotiable, but is likely to include: the deposit for every lot which it is anticipated that the client will be trading, an element to cover commissions, and an element to cover possible short-term variation margins. It might be, for example, that a client who wishes to place a 50 lot hedge on a market whose ICCH minimum deposit is US$250, but who has

agreed to pay double ICCH minimum, would deposit $40,000. (50 × $500 = $25,000 + $15,000 extra to cover commissions and small variation margins.)

(2) The moment that the client trades, his account will be debited the initial deposit (say $500 per lot) plus the agreed commission. The commission agreed will normally be so much per lot "round turn" (i.e., to buy and sell one lot).

(3) The client's open position (i.e., the number of lots which he has bought but not yet sold, or sold but not yet bought back) will be valued by the broker at the official closing price every evening. His account will be debited by the amount that the market has moved against him. If that overdraws his account, the broker will make a "variation margin call". He will ask the client to pay an amount of money probably immediately (or at least within an agreed time). If the client does not do so, the broker has the right to "close out" the position—he is entitled to sell some of the lots which the client has bought or buy back some which he has sold. If the market has moved against the client only temporarily, this will quite clearly be against his better interests. This is why it is in the client's interest to keep the broker in more than adequate funds. (Many brokers will pay interest on free money held with them).

Let us work through an actual freight futures example.

A charterer hedger wishes to buy 50 lots of April futures at 1,400. He opens an account with a BIFFEX broker by signing an account opening form and risk disclosure statement. He agrees with the broker that he will pay double deposit ($500 per lot) and a round turn commission of $40 per lot. The broker agrees to pay interest at 1.5% below base rate on any free money held with him.

Day 1	*Balance*
The hedger opens his account with	$35,000 CR
The broker buys 50 lots at 1,500	
Deposit 50 × $500 = $25,000	$10,000 CR
Commission 50 × $40 = $2,000	$8,000 CR
Closing price = 1,500 (Unchanged)	
Closing balance =	$8,000 CR

Day 2
Closing price = 1,510
(open position has increased in value by 10 points
= $100 per lot = $5,000) $5,000 CR
Closing balance = $13,000 CR

Day 5
Closing price = 1,450
(open position has decreased in value by 60 points
= $600 per lot = $30,000) $30,000 DR
Closing balance = $17,000 DR

Day 6
Variation Margin Call = $17,000
Client pays = $20,000 CR
Closing balance = $3,000 CR

Day 75
Charterer fixes ship and sells hedge at 1,650

Final position

Bought 50 lots at 1,500
Sold 50 lots at 1,650
Profit per lot = 150 × $10 = $1,500
Total profit $1,500 × 50 = $75,000
Plus initial deposit = $35,000
Plus negative variation call = $17,000
Total value = $130,500
Plus interest earned = $750
                                                     ─────────
                                                     $129,750

Less commissions
50 × $40 =   2,000
Client's account $127,750 CR

To recap, there are really four main elements in the financial relationship between the futures user and (via his broker) the clearing system. They are:

(a) Initial margin or deposits

This is a variable good-faith deposit, a minimum figure being set by the clearing house but the client often paying a pre-agreed multiple of that minimum. The deposit is a product of the volatility of the market, and is usually at least enough to cover one day's movement. The deposit is returnable when you close the position out.

(b) Variation margin or maintenance margin

Your positions will be "marked to market" every night—in other words revalued at the official closing price. You will then be required to pay whatever losses your position might have incurred.

(c) Commission

This is usually a per lot figure agreed with your broker. It will normally be expressed as a "round turn"—i.e., the commission required to buy and then sell one lot. You may be able to negotiate commission rebates of one sort or another. Some brokers will charge a lower commission for spreads or straddles or for day-trades. A broker may agree a volume rebate if you are a very large volume trader.

(d) Finance, interest and cash-flow

Most normally you will be required to finance your futures trading in cash and in advance. Some brokers may agree credit terms with a suitably large and credit-worthy client. Normally you will be advised to maintain excess funds in your account with your broker to cover short-term adverse movements, and to avoid the constant transfer of small sums of money. Most brokers will pay interest on free money in the account, sometimes on unrealised paper profits. The level of interest will never be as good as you would achieve in a bank but will be designed to give you some incentive to maintain excess funds in your account. Many brokers will pay, for example, the London overnight rate less 1%, and will charge on any short-term deficit the overnight rate plus 1%.

Most elements of the financial relationship between the broker and his client are negotiable, but this is probably a reasonable indication of the most normal scenario.

In general, the most important part of a successful futures trading experience is the application of a series of financial and trading disciplines. It would be foolish to pretend that there are no pitfalls inherent in the highly-geared and fast-moving futures markets, but a highly-disciplined approach such as that suggested should avoid most of them, and enable the hedger successfully to offset the risk he is facing in his real market.

CHAPTER 11

MAKING MONEY WITH FUTURES

Much printer's ink and a fair proportion of an Amazonian rain forest has so far been expended explaining the purpose of futures and options—the use of the markets to offset or manage risk as an adjunct to a company's real underlying business. And it is very right that it should be so. For hedging in its many guises is the only ultimate purpose of a futures market. If a futures market is not performing a real trade need—if it is allowed to become a casino, or if the prices become excessively divorced from the underlying reality of the market—then there is no point in having it. Not only that, but every futures market in history which has been allowed to degenerate into a punter's paradise has ultimately withered away and died. So it is right that a book such as this—and indeed the exchange authorities, in presentations and seminars—should concentrate on the trade hedging uses of a futures market.

Having said that, an essential element in any futures market will always be speculation. For whereas the hedger is in essence trying to remove risk the speculator clearly likes risk. He hopes to make a profit out of accepting the risk which the hedger is trying to remove. This is why futures markets are often referred to as risk transference media—they are used to transfer risk from the risk-averse hedger to the risk-hungry speculator.

Not only are speculators needed to accept the risk which the hedger is trying to remove, but they also provide an essential service in assuring the liquidity of the futures market. They do this in several ways. First, in many markets most professional trade users tend to hear the same piece of news or come to the same conclusion about the likely direction of the market at the same time. Thus if there were only professional or trade participants, the market would become illiquid—would tend to move rapidly in one direction without trading. But speculators will always be there to take the opposite view, either because they are not aware of what is happening in the market in question or because they are trying to spot "a turn", or perhaps simply because they feel the price has gone far enough in one direction and they now wish to "take a profit" on an existing position. The most fundamental rule of all futures trading is that there is always a price for everything. You may not want to sell me your house for £10,000, but you would move out tomorrow for £1 million. Somewhere between the two there is a fair market price which will be higher or lower depending on the relative strength of your desire to sell and my desire to buy. The speculator—whether private client, professional speculator or futures fund—ensures that there will always be a price of some kind available in the futures market.

THE AIM OF THE SPECULATOR

So what are the speculator's aims, methods and practices? This chapter will attempt to introduce some of them. The speculator aims, of course to make money out of his futures trading activity. This aim is in sharp contradistinction to the hedger, whose main aim is to remove risk for his underlying business, even if that may cost a premium. In other words, the hedger may under some circumstances be happy, or at least prepared, to lose money on the futures market, since that in itself indicates that the underlying market is performing more favourably than he would have expected. In other words, his futures losses could be viewed as an insurance premium on a policy against an adverse market move—a policy against which he is looking less and less likely to make a claim. (The only flaw in this old analogy of the insurance market being that in futures the premium becomes larger and larger the less he needs the policy—options are more directly analogous to insurance.) At any rate, the investor, the speculator, the punter—call him what you will—is different to the hedger. His only motivation is the making of a profit by taking a particular position on a futures market.

As in any other market, the speculator on the futures market aims to buy any of the contract months, expecting them to go up in price, to sell them prior to a fall, or to buy one contract and sell another expecting the differential in price between them either to narrow or to widen (spreads, straddles or switches). There is no great mystery about the speculator's methods. He takes a view of what the physical market will be at one of the settlement dates, or more probably what is likely to happen to the futures prices in the meanwhile, and buys or sells accordingly. He comes to his conclusion about the market in a combination of three ways. He analyses the supply and demand of the commodity and of the various reasons for that balance altering (this is called fundamental analysis); he analyses movements in the futures prices, and draws conclusions about the way they are likely to move in the future (this is called technical analysis); or he operates on the basis of a pure marketman's "gut-feel" of which way the prices are going to go.

Fundamental analysis

Fundamental analysis of a market is the normal econometric analysis with which most businessmen will be familiar. The statistics relating to the supply of the commodity will very often be readily available. If not, a variety of governmental bodies (or Quangos) are always ready to provide analysis of the acreage sown in the Ukraine, the pumping capacity of the OPEC countries or the US Government's debt requirements (which respectively provide the supply side statistics for grain, crude oil and US T-Bond futures). The demand side is often more difficult to analyse since it may involve subjective views or guesses of such issues as future weather patterns, military developments in the Middle East, and political strictures on the US Government's handling of the economy (in each of our three examples respectively). Nonetheless it is usually possible to come to some kind of view of likely forward patterns of demand for most commodities.

Fundamental analysis and the resulting speculative recommendations are quite simply based on the arithmetic calculation of supply less demand. Clearly, the smaller the surplus the higher the price is likely to be. Or at least that is true if all of the other speculators have access to the same statistical data as you do. But bearing in mind that many of the statistics for both supply and demand may well rest on fairly subjective estimates, it will be clear that there is no such thing as an absolutely certain prediction of forward supply and demand. If there was, there would be no futures market, since it would take merely a straightforward arithmetic calculation to work out what the price should be.

So clearly while a firm grasp of the fundamentals of supply and demand are a necessary prerequisite of successful speculation on any market, they should not necessarily be relied on too slavishly. They are at best a start point for further analysis of the market in question.

Technical analysis

Whereas fundamental analysis may seem fairly obvious to the layman, technical analysis, which is the second main way of attempting to predict likely movements in futures markets, may well seem a great deal more arcane, and tends to meet a degree of wary scepticism from the lay observer. So what is technical analysis? In essence, it is analysis of charts or graphs of historic price movements (either physical or futures prices) and the attempt to extrapolate those movements into predictions about likely future movements. And at its simplest there is an obvious logic in this. Whereas printed pages of statistics are virtually meaningless, their presentation in graphic form tells an obvious story. The following graphs, for example, are very clear:

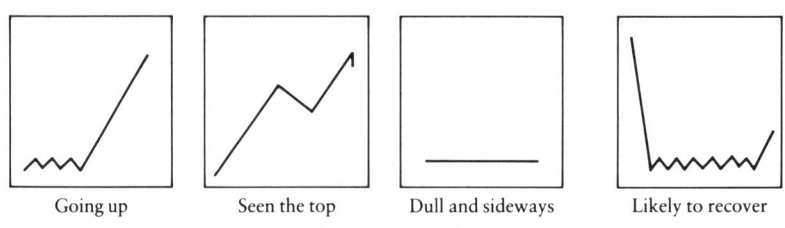

| Going up | Seen the top | Dull and sideways | Likely to recover |

Figure 21. Technical analysis examples

You don't have to be a statistical genius to see that these predictions are overall likely to be correct. (Although of course any market can astound all of us, whether we are fundamental or technical analysts, by doing exactly the opposite to what everyone expects.)

AIM OF SPECULATOR

By looking at these charts and coming to some form of view about the likely further movement of the market, we are applying a very basic and unsophisticated form of technical analysis to whichever markets these may be.

By increasing the degree of sophistication of our analysis, we are basically improving the statistical likelihood of our prediction being correct. There are really two main areas in which technical analysis achieves this: first by learning to recognise certain patterns of price action which have tended in the past to indicate a certain type of price action to come. Trend lines, double bottoms or tops, head and shoulders, flags, pennants, triangles are all examples of chart patterns which technical analysts look out for and from which they attempt to predict the future. Areas of "support" (below which there is a low statistical likelihood of a fall) or of "overhead resistance" (which the market is unlikely to breach on the upside) are naturally particularly important.

After chart patterns, the other area of statistical sophistication which improves basic technical analysis is what are known as momentum indicators. These indicators in essence use "moving averages" of the prices (i.e., charts not of the prices themselves but of a continuing average of daily price moves, which smooths out short-term troughs or peaks) to assess the speed with which a market is moving in a particular direction. Such analysis produces the relative strength indicator (RSI) and stochastic, the complexities of both of which, and of the other sophisticated technical analysis techniques, are well beyond the scope of this book.

Suffice to say that your futures broker should be able to supply you with analysis of the price action depicted on a chart, from which he will be drawing conclusions based on accepted and recognisable chart functions and on various measurements of the velocity and momentum of historic price change. It is very easy to fall into the trap of being excessively cynical about all of this—to dismiss it as fairytales and poppycock and to ask for your crystal ball. But it is in reality much less fanciful and much more scientific than the layman might at first think. After all, it is merely a branch of statistics and should therefore be fairly scientific. It may be interesting to note that the largest single speculative element in the futures markets today is the huge professionally-managed futures funds, that they rely primarily on technical analysis and trade on the trends in the markets, and that they tend to average an annual return in excess of 20%, and often as high as 100% or more. Technical analysis really does work, and must not be too lightly dismissed.

Making trading decisions

So armed with a battery of statistics about the supply and demand of the commodity or financial instrument in question and with a portfolio of up-to-the-minute charts of historic price action heavily overscored with your favourite technical analyst's remarks about "inverted head and shoulders pattern", "double bottoms", "island reversals" or "ascending pennants", how do you actually decide what to do? Which of this massive array of information should you give most weight to?

Well, clearly if the fundamental analysis and technical analysis say the same thing at the same time, there is a high degree of likelihood that they will be right. If the fundamental analysis is giving you a strong message in one direction or another, I would tend to follow that, even if the technicals seem to be against it. You inevitably have to come to a decision based on your feel for the market—do the prices *seem* too low or too high? Are you more convinced by the fundamental or the technical analysis? Above all, what is the balance of probabilities? In chapter one we touched briefly on risk/reward analysis. But it is here as a speculator that it really comes into its own. Always be aware what the risk involved in a particular investment strategy is, compared to the targeted reward. Be quite analytical and strict about this—"I am risking £100. If the market goes the way I expect it will, I will make £1,000. My risk/reward ratio is 1/10". And apply strict trading disciplines to make sure that you lock that risk/reward ratio in.

The application of strict trading disciplines is perhaps even more important if you are a speculator rather than a hedger. For losses caused by slack or unprofessional trading are completely unacceptable to the speculator—the hedger may well find ways of explaining small losses away.

"Stop loss" trading is particularly important here. If you are buying London Wheat at £100 a tonne with a target of £110, and the technical and fundamental analysis encourages you in this view, how far are you prepared to let the market move against you in the meanwhile? To £98? or £95? or £90? Somewhere there is a level

AIM OF SPECULATOR

below which you cannot and will not go, either because you cannot face the adverse variation margin calls or because you come to realise that your original view and expectation was, with hindsight, wrong. The important point is to decide that level in advance. While buying wheat at £100, with a £110 target, set a stop loss level, either for yourself or better by placing a "Good Till Cancelled" (GTC) order with your broker. While placing an order such as "Pay £100 for 100 Sept wheat", add: "If done sell 100 Sept wheat at £98 on stop GTC, OCO (one cancels the other) sell 100 Sept wheat at £110 GTC". You are formalising your belief that the market will go to £110, but that if it moves £2 against you, you want out. You are formalising the risk/reward ratio at 2/10. Stop loss trading like this (and in a few more sophisticated forms) is a very useful way of applying the trading disciplines outlined in the last chapter. It takes a certain amount of practice and experience. For example, the "stop" level must not be so close to the market that the stop gets triggered at just the wrong time (i.e., if the market moves temporarily against you). One of the worst experiences in the futures world is being stopped out at the wrong time. At the same time the stop level must clearly be close enough to the current market to make sure that you do get out of an adverse movement before it is too damaging.

Don't forget that the gearing inherent in the margining system implies the potential for large losses as well as huge gains. Since all you are actually paying up front is a deposit equivalent to something like 5% of the value of the commodity which you are buying or selling, a 5% move against you wipes out your investment. A 10% move against you (which is pretty modest in some of these markets) means that you lose your investment and the same again. A 20% movement implies some pretty massive losses.

The gearing and risk of speculative investment in the futures markets should not, however, put you off. The advantages are in direct proportion to the risks, and some futures exposure is therefore sensible in any investment portfolio. But the risk does mean that an individual trading account, with the client taking his own trading decisions and merely placing orders with his futures broker, may not be suitable for the non-expert.

In that case, a number of alternatives exist. First, most brokers will probably offer some form of "Individual Managed Portfolio", whereby the broker takes the trading decisions on your behalf, often in accordance with a previously agreed risk profile or trading plan.

It may be that the broker will offer a service whereby he invests part of your funds automatically in each of the broker's analyst's recommendations. He may offer a specialist investment programme (for example, specialising in "spreads" with a more limited risk profile than straight positions). And he may well offer you an account which combines some of these specialist areas.

An increasingly important area of investment in the futures market comes from the "futures funds". These are currently mainly offshore funds which attract investors on the basis of historic performance by the fund's "CTAs" (Commodity Trading Advisors). If currently planned changes in UK tax and regulatory regime become law, such funds will increasingly be traded (and marketed) onshore, and will increasingly become tradable in the same way as equity unit trusts.

Another popular type of fund is what is known as the "Guaranteed fund". Ordinary non-guaranteed futures funds theoretically suffer from the same risk as the private futures trading account—that it is perfectly possible to lose the entire initial investment, possibly even more. As an antidote to this some brokers offer what are known as "Guaranteed funds", whereby they guarantee to return the capital at the end of a set period. They do this by means of investing say 75% of the capital in fixed-interest bonds of one kind or another, calculated to return the capital to 100% within the stipulated period, and then they invest the balance of 25% in the futures markets. There are clear attractions in this form of fund, although in a sense the investor could achieve a similar end by investing the 75% in gilts and bonds himself, and then applying suitable trading disciplines to the balance in the futures markets.

The broker will be happy to tailor your investments to your own criteria—high, middling or low risk, or guaranteed; with you taking all, some or none of the trading decisions, and the aim being capital growth or (more rarely) an income flow. Like any other investment adviser, the professional futures broker will find ways of tailoring his product to your needs. The important thing from your point of view is to make sure that you are being looked after by an adviser of a size, integrity and reputation to make you wholly comfortable with leaving large sums of money with him.

It is always worth remembering, whether you are trading for yourself or using a broker's funds or recommendations, that there are more commodities millionaires around than almost any other type of millionaire. There are also more commodities bankrupts. It is clearly important to diversify part of your investment portfolio into the exciting and highly lucrative futures markets, but equally undeniable that they should be "handled with care".

CHAPTER 12

THE FUTURE FOR FUTURES

1. THE 'EIGHTIES : THATCHERITE EXPANSION AFTER 'SEVENTIES INFLATION

The use of futures, options and other derivatives for the scientific management of risk has been one of the most dazzling developments of the 'eighties. In 1979 when the Thatcher Government came to power we were suffering from rampant inflation, high interest rates, exchange controls, industry racked by division and inefficiency, and the derivatives markets in the City of London were—with hindsight—remarkably unsophisticated. The 'seventies had been the period of huge success in the London commodities (metals, cocoa, coffee, sugar and so on) markets. Not only did exchange controls prevent the export of risk-seeking capital but inflationary pressures made the purchase of physical commodities a highly attractive investment.

But removal of exchange controls, deregulation, Big Bang, the Financial Services Act and a lot of other Thatcherite developments and enactments in the 'eighties have transformed the derivatives markets of the City of London beyond recognition. First in 1982/83 came the development of financial futures (based on new thinking coming from Chicago) and the establishment of LIFFE, the London International Financial Futures Exchange. LIFFE's expansion since has been explosive and dramatic, and after its amalgamation in 1990 with the London Traded Options Market, LTOM, to create LDE, the London Derivatives Exchange, it will be by far the largest and most dynamic market in Europe. It is still dwarfed by the massive Chicago Exchanges, but if the pace of its development in the 'eighties were extrapolated into the 'nineties it would soon come to rival the mighty CBOT and CME (Chicago's Board of Trade and Mercantile Exchange).

It was the 'eighties, too, which saw the foundation and growth of the International Petroleum Exchange (IPE), trading initially a highly successful gas oil contract, and by the end of the decade a fast-expanding cash-settled Brent Crude oil contract, an as-yet embyronic heavy fuel oil contract, and a Dubai sour crude contract.

The old London Terminal Markets in cocoa, coffee and sugar amalgamated in the 'eighties to create the LCE (London Commodities Exchange), now renamed London FOX (London Futures and Options Exchange) and housed in its own purpose-built premises in Commodity Quay in St Katharine Docks. (The inappropriateness of its name is apparently lost on the City-dwellers who inhabit Commodity Quay.)

In the Metals world, the 'eighties saw one of the worst crises to hit the futures industry ever—the tin crisis—created, as so many problems are, by Governmental commodity pacts and similar interference in the operation of free markets. But in retrospect the tin crisis was less damaging to the futures industry (with one or two noticeable exceptions) than it might have been, and than some people thought at the time it was going to be. And by forcing the LME (London Metals Exchange) towards use of the Common Clearing System offered by ICCH the crisis may even have provided a useful service.

The LME conducts a massive amount of business and remains the premier metals market in the world. But its self-confessed status as a trade market primarily for conducting real physical business, rather than as a cash-paper market place like a true futures exchange, whose main purpose is risk-transference, has always meant that the LME is somewhat out on a limb of its own.

Alongside these highly significant developments in the main London futures exchanges (and the equally exciting developments which were simultaneously occurring elsewhere in the world), the Baltic Futures Exchange, too, underwent a series of quite significant changes. Not only did the BFE develop a highly successful potato futures contract (potatoes are one of the most volatile commodities in the world), not only did it attract in the Soya Bean Meal Futures Contract and invent the concept of meat futures (pigs, which are now cash-settled, and live cattle, which is currently dormant), but it also provided a home for the development of BIFFEX. Freight Futures, of course, is one of the most innovative creations of the 'eighties. It is now the only contract of its kind in the world (the

INTEX experiment failed largely because of the high cost of the technology involved), it is the only futures contract based on a service rather than a commodity or financial instrument, it is the only futures contract which is physically collocated with its underlying cash commodity—shipping, which of course is traded on the floor of the Baltic Exchange. It is a mystery—at least to me—why BIFFEX has not so far been more successful than it has. (This is an important issue which will be addressed in the next chapter.)

The Baltic Futures Exchange has also led the way by amalgamating five entirely separate futures markets—BIFFEX, the London Potato Futures Association, the London Soya Bean Meal Futures Association, the London Meat Futures Association and GAFTA (the Grain and Feed Trade Association) grain futures contract. This amalgamation was forced on the BFE by the 1987 Financial Services Act (FSA), which required all futures markets to be registered with the Securities and Investments Board (SIB) as Regulated Investment Exchanges (RIEs). (Everything in the futures industry seems to be denominated by the Three-letter Mnemonic, or TLM as it is known.) So the FSA forced the BFE to become an RIE reporting to the SIB (via that well-known FLM, the AFBD, which is in the process of amalgamating with TSA—the Association of Futures Brokers and Dealers and The Securities Association to the uninitiated).

The BFE has since taken that regulatory amalgamation of its five separate markets further into a physical amalgamation by creating one trading area on the floor of the Baltic Exchange. From all of this other London markets, who seem to spend their time competing with one another, could take a lesson. Even the misappropriately named London FOX, which has brought the three terminal market associations together under one nominal umbrella, has still left each of them with a large degree of independence and autonomy, and has signally failed to persuade them to collocate to one floor. The existing bizarre arrangement on the London FOX floor in Commodity Quay whereby the markets are in roughly the same place but divided by glass partitions is neither one thing nor t'other. If reason ever prevails, coffee, cocoa and sugar will come together in a proper pit trading system on one floor; more about this below.

So the 'eighties saw some spectacular developments in all of London's derivatives markets and saw the foundations being laid for a truly professional, truly international London-based futures industry for the 'nineties.

2. THE 'NINETIES: THE EXPECTED AND THE DESIRABLE

So what can we now be looking forward to? What developments are imminent, and what developments, if not imminent, should we be working towards to ensure the continued healthy development of the London futures industry?

First, the 'nineties seem destined to witness further explosive expansion of the derivatives markets in general. More and more industries are beginning to understand the need for risk management using futures and options, and are becoming increasingly sophisticated and familiar with their use. Not only will we therefore see a huge increase in volume and liquidities of existing contracts, but we are also likely to see the development of entirely new contracts and types of investment. Plans are already afoot for a whole variety of European interest-rate contracts, for electricity, property, high-protein soyabean meal, tanker freights, tea, rice, reinsurance, apples, eggs, a European Stock Index, Arabica Coffee, diamonds, gold and sheep-meat, no doubt among other, even more abstruse, commodities. Some of these will never be launched, others will be launched but never trade successfully, one or two may turn out to be the sort of success that the German Bund and Brent Crude oil contracts have been.

London FOX are currently being particularly active in their search for and development of new contracts. They may even be in danger of doing too many things in too short a time, and failing properly to develop an environment within which these new ideas stand a chance of flying.

Launching a new contract is one of the most difficult and uncertain ventures ever undertaken. Quite the most extraordinary contracts seem to do well, while other "obvious candidates" fall at the first fence.

In broad terms, three things seem to me to be essential for a new contract to succeed:

> First, reasonable demand from the industry in question, who perceive some part of their business to entail an unacceptable risk. It is absolutely pointless for an exchange to

think up some clever contract and then attempt to foist it on an unwilling user community. The initiative must come from the industry.

Secondly, a carefully constructed contract is clearly necessary. The commodity traded must be instantly recognisable as a benchmark or yardstick by the underlying industry. For it to succeed, a futures contract must either exactly match the hedger's own commodity or have a direct and obvious (and reasonably constant) relationship with it.

Thirdly (and this last element is crucial) the exchange involved must provide a trading environment within which the contract stands a chance of succeeding. End users put together in some kind of exchange environment will always be unlikely to create a vibrant market. Both buyers and sellers will have exaggerated ideas of the price they want to achieve and they will stare at each other across an unbridgeable divide—a real Mexican stand-off. You need brokers, jobbers, "locals" as they are called, speculators, funds and the rest to bridge that gap, to create the liquidity which the end user needs. Not only that, but since no futures contract is ever likely to be embraced so quickly and so completely by the industry which it serves that it becomes instantly liquid, an enthusiastic broking community who are ready and able to put their backs into selling the contract is an essential prerequisite.

The successful launch of a new futures product needs good demand from the industry for a risk-management investment; the correct contract trading an instantly recognisable commodity; and a committed and enthusiastic broking community dedicated to getting the contract off the ground.

These various elements exist in supreme form in the Chicago and New York markets, and to a very good degree on LIFFE. The London Commodities Markets (IPE, FOX, BFE, LME) are all very good at thinking up new contracts (although not always with the support of the industry), but have not yet been successful in creating a critical mass of futures brokers able and willing to get a new contract going (the Brent Crude contract on IPE is a signal exception).

So the first development in the 'nineties will be a huge growth in volume of existing contracts together with the development of a wide variety of new futures products. This expansion will probably be aided by another likely development: the growth in over-the-counter tailor-made derivative products suitable for the end-user.

For futures contracts are by definition particular and specialised. They trade a yardstick or benchmark commodity of a highly specific grade and delivery. By definition, such a commodity will not always satisfy the end-user. For example, airlines, shipping companies and power generators all have huge exposure to the fluctuations in the oil price. But the differences between the particular oils which they trade and those traded on the futures markets prevent them taking out a very successful hedge using futures. An increasingly popular solution to this problem of "basis risk" is the use of tailor-made derivative instruments such as OTC options, swaps, swaptions, collars and caps. Using these increasingly-complex instruments a market-maker or financial institution either takes the risk on its own book, taking a view on the underlying market, or does a "back-to-back" deal with another client who is trying to remove the opposite risk (e.g. the airline company and the jet-fuel producer); or they may lay off the risk on a regulated futures exchange. In other words the intermediary who is an expert in these things makes his money out of managing the basis risk which is unacceptable to the end-user.

If the trend continues—which seems very likely—specialist over-the-counter derivative instruments seem destined to continue their rapid growth, backed up by expanding futures markets which will develop an increasingly wholesale appearance.

This will mean a declining importance for small, specialised futures contracts offering a specialist service to a particular trade. For they will increasingly be looking to specialist institutions to provide a series of ever-more-complex risk management instruments carefully tailored to their own particular needs. But the usage of the large fast-moving fully-liquid futures contracts traded on the world's major exchanges will benefit hugely.

There is already a discernible trend away from the trade-related specialist contracts and exchanges typified in London by FOX and BFE towards the cash-settled, high-volume, fully-liquid approach of LIFFE and IPE. This move from "commodities markets" to "futures markets" seems destined to continue apace into the 'nineties, and it is a movement which the exchanges and their members must embrace and encourage if they are to continue and prosper.

For example, it is particularly absurd that we currently have six futures and options exchanges here in London (LIFFE, LTOM, LME, FOX, IPE, BFE). Some of these are already amalgamations of old one-contract exchanges, of which there were probably something like 15 in existence in London as recently as five years or so ago. The duplication of effort of management, marketing, compliance, systems and so on by the exchanges is matched by the demonstrable inefficiency of the large brokerage companies having six separate floor operations.

There are already some moves afoot to remedy this. LIFFE and LTOM have already announced their intention to merge into a renamed London Derivatives Exchange, and to relocate from the Royal Exchange and from the old Stock Exchange respectively to a purpose-built trading floor above Cannon Street Station. How sensible it would be if we could persuade the commodities markets (LME, FOX, IPE and BFE) similarly to merge and to collocate. Perhaps if (as I suspect) the political rivalries, the self-protective attitudes of Boards and officials, and the endemic inertia and apathy of many of the members of the London exchanges are sufficient to prevent such an amalgamation, then at least the coming together on one central floor under a loose federation of some kind might be the next best thing. Perhaps the Bank of England should take the initiative in establishing an entirely new entity, the European Commodities Exchange (why do we continue to insist on maintaining the narrow parochialism inherent in calling everything the "London —— Exchange"?). Each of the four mercantile or commodities exchanges could then affiliate itself to the new body and make use of certain centralised functions (marketing, PR, trade registrations and other computer systems, telecommunications and compliance are all obvious areas which would benefit from co-operation), but, if they wish, maintain independent control of their own ultimate destinies, perhaps such things as contract development and even perhaps the precise method of trading.

The European Commodities Exchange need not necessarily be collocated with the London Derivatives Exchange. The Cannon-bridge Development looks like taking a very long time for completion and will certainly cost a fortune, and the mutual collocation of all of London's markets would produce a huge and unwieldy multi-headed monster. Big is not necessarily beautiful in this context. What's more, it could reasonably be argued that there is actually very little in common between financial futures and equities and index options on the one hand and commodity futures on the other. They have the name "futures" and the general principle in common, but there is no real evidence from other markets that short-sterling traders will be willing or able at a moment's notice to jump into the soyabean meal pit and start trading.

Those who are calling for the complete merger of all of London's markets may be a little naive. A quicker, cheaper, cleaner solution may well be collocation of FOX, IPE, Baltic, possibly even LME on one large pit-trading floor under a federation of some kind. Where that floor should be is open to debate. Commodity Quay is an obvious candidate, as long as the cocoa, coffee and sugar markets can be persuaded to come out of their fishbowls and take part in a proper futures exchange floor. Alternatives may be the Royal Exchange, shortly to be vacated by LIFFE, or perhaps even the Baltic Exchange. The Baltic has a number of advantages: a superb central location, a prestigious (and freehold and therefore comparatively cheap) building, huge quantities of office space, restaurants, wine bars, telecommunications facilities and the rest. It also has a listed floor which is being used less and less by the shipping community and would lend itself superbly to futures trading.

Whilst an amalgamation of commodities exchanges trading on a proper pit-type basis on a remodelled Baltic floor sounds a perfect solution to many of London's ills, however, it would be a brave (or foolish) politician who would attempt to make such a dream reality. The entrenched attitudes, self-interest, arrogance, and lethargy of some of the institutions and individuals concerned in such a move might well preclude it.

But if as a result of our inability to make such a dream reality we find in five years' time that London has lost its primacy as a commodity futures centre, that some of our excellent contracts have dwindled away, that more of our futures brokers have gone out of business, and that we are being outstripped by new commodity exchanges in Paris or Frankfurt, then we will have no-one to blame but ourselves.*

---

*Since writing this section, BFE and FOX have announced that they intend to merge: this is applauded and recommended to IPE and LME—the only exchanges now left on their own.

3. THE TWENTY-FIRST CENTURY, OR SOONER?

There is one development which seems certain fundamentally to change the futures industry as a whole over the next ten years or so—the development of computerised trading systems. There is a school of thought which believes the open outcry floor system of trading to be clumsy, inefficient, antiquated and open to abuse, and which advocates trading via a computer terminal as an alternative. And there is clearly quite a lot to recommend automated trading. It is quick, efficient, cheap, spreads the geographic coverage of the exchange wider, permits extended trading hours and so on. And numerous exchanges are experimenting with automated trading at the moment.

There are in essence two main types of automated trading system: Those, like LIFFE's APT (Automated Pit Trading) and CBOT's Aurora which aim to replicate exactly the liquidity, trading methods and membership structure of existing pit-traded exchanges. The exponents of pit-replication denigrate the alternative as "merely" order-matching systems in which buy orders and sell orders are listed, and if opposite orders appear they are matched and a trade takes place. The granddaddy of automated trading systems, INTEX (which, incidentally, traded the only other freight futures contract ever to exist), was an order-matching system. So is the system developed by ICCH, called ATS and ATS II (Automated Trading Systems) and used for some years by the New Zealand Futures Exchange, by Dublin's IFOX and until recently by London FOX to offer a white sugar contract. London FOX now uses an order-matching system called FAST originally developed by the Sydney Futures Exchange.

Elsewhere in the world, the Chicago Mercantile Exchange in partnership with Reuters and now with CBOT have developed a system called Globex. This will be a truly worldwide order-matching system offering contracts currently traded on CME, CBOT and the Paris Financial Futures Exchange, Matif. Globex is said also to be in negotiation with other worldwide exchanges, and looks set to develop a commanding presence in the world's automated markets. Elsewhere, OM, the Swedish equities options exchange, has gone Europe-wide on a computer, and Germany has already launched equity options and will shortly launch futures on its own system, DTB. Switzerland has SOFFEX, and most other

European countries seem to be on the verge of launching their own domestic futures exchanges using screens.

So what are we to make of the development of automated trading? Well first of all, it is coming, and there is nothing we can do to turn the tide back. We must learn to harness the new technology to our own ends. Make it our slave, not our master.

Secondly, it does indeed have a very useful role to play, particularly in the reasonably cost-effective expansion of trading hours and in the geographic widening of an exchange's membership.

Thirdly, there is a strong move by the regulators of the world's futures exchanges towards encouraging automated trading in the (perhaps mistaken) belief that they are easier to regulate than pits. It is important that they do not get carried away by the velocity of their own exuberance and force a too-speedy transfer to screens. If handled badly this could have very serious implications for liquidity and volume.

Fourthly, there are a number of powerful interest groups, particularly the computer manufacturers and vendors (Reuters, Telerate and so on), who would have a clear commercial reason for pushing the industry towards automation. High technology can sometimes develop a life and a momentum all of its own.

Fifthly, other interest groups, such as the large Futures Commission Merchants in the US and perhaps end-users who are currently futures brokers' clients, may become convinced that they have something to gain from automated trading. They should beware of being persuaded of this by the salesmen without properly investigating the real consequences of closing the pits.

And sixthly, there may indeed be an inevitability about the move to screen trading. The history of technology indicates that it nearly always triumphs. I have a bet with one of our directors in GNI that there will be no major futures exchanges still operating on open outcry floors by the end of the century. I believe that that will be the case, although I am not necessarily an advocate of it.

For I am convinced by the argument that a large part of the liquidity and volume of the world's most active futures contracts is provided by the very inefficiency of the open outcry system. If all of the players had access to the same information at precisely the same moment, and if all they had to do to cancel their futures orders was to hit a switch, the futures markets would by definition become "one-way". Added to that, very few locals or jobbers would be able to operate effectively on a screen. At the present state of the technology screen trading seems much less likely to achieve a high degree of liquidity than open outcry. That may well change if and when voice-activation technology, whereby a computer will react instantly and 100% efficiently and accurately to a trader's voice, achieves a reasonable degree of development. For when that happens traders, brokers, locals and jobbers alike will once again be trading by open outcry, albeit they are invisible to one another and trading from the comfort of their own dealing rooms. Voice Activation Technology is currently something like 30% effective, when orders are given in a flat, even voice—clearly useless in the highly charged and erratic atmosphere of a busy dealing room. But if the demand is there, the boffins will assuredly overcome the difficulties and develop the appropriate technology.

So we should beware of regulators and vendors who advocate screen trading to the exclusion of the floors straight away; those luddites who will not contemplate any form of automated trading are worse. We must learn to harness the technology to our ends, and avoid the temptation to throw the baby out with the bathwater.

One last thing here: If the development of automated trading is taken to its logical development, particularly using voice-activation, it would be perfectly possible to end up in a situation perhaps not dissimilar to the Stock Exchange's use of automated trading, whereby end-users effectively have direct access to each other on a screen. While there may be apparent advantages in this for the end-user, it would almost certainly result in a huge reduction in liquidity. The enthusiasm, hard work, market analysis, broking skills and other value-added services of the futures broker, as well as the market-making skills of the jobber and local, are absolutely necessary to ensure a contract's success. Reduce or remove the broker's profitability and the local's trading environment and you will without doubt kill the markets. End-users beware.

If the 'seventies were the era of inflation-led and exchange-control-fed expansion of London's Commodities markets and the 'eighties built on that to develop financial and energy futures, the 'nineties seem set to be the era of consolidation among futures exchanges, of massive further expansion of volumes and liquidity (despite or because of the end-user's increasing tendency towards more tailor-made investments than futures can ever be), of the development of all kinds of new contracts and products, and of the increasing use of trading technology.

The futures industry will be a wholly changed business by the year 2000. Wholly changed, but no doubt just as dynamic and exciting a business as it has always been.

CHAPTER 13

SHIPPING MARKET RISK : TOWARDS A NEW ERA

In the first edition of this book, written it will be remembered at the low point of the shipping slump of the mid-eighties, I wrote:

> Discussion on how we can extricate ourselves from the present crisis in the shipping industry, whether that be by increasing scrapping levels, decreasing new building levels, changing trading patterns or tonnage ownership patterns or whatever will go on for a very long time. Risk management can play only a small part in that recovery. As an industry, we have taken unacceptable risks, we have gambled our all on the commercial roulette wheel, which has finally come up at nought. (Although the bank, on this occasion, does not appear to have won either.)
>
> Where skilful use of risk-management, of hedging in its various guises, will come fully into its own will be after the crisis has passed, when we must try to avoid such a catastrophe again. The industry is going to have to come to terms with the fact that the old tradition of an entrepreneur borrowing on his reputation and projected cash flows to finance new tonnage, and then tramping the vessel on the spot market, taking trading decisions more or less by guess and by God, is finished for ever. The same quantity of cargo (inflated only by growth in the World economy) will have to be moved over roughly the same number of sea miles, but the tonnage which moves it is going to have to be much better managed in commercial terms if the industry as a whole is to thrive and prosper. And the skilful management of the risks of the shipping business will be a critically important part of that exercise.
>
> As we said in Chapter 1, a large part of the profit potential in shipping comes from the risk inherent in the business, but the days of the haphazard pursuit of profits by means of raw, unfettered risk are gone. The secure future of the industry lies in the timely and skilful calculation of risk/reward ratios, followed by shrewd and sophisticated use of one of the variety of risk management tools available to shipowner, charterer, operator, trader, grower, producer and end user alike.

The development of freight futures, and the growth and increasing use of oil and financial futures as hedging mediums are timely. The necessity to restructure the industry on a sound commercial basis is apparent to all. It is the view of the author that increased usage of futures hedging should be at least one main element in that restructuring. If the industry as a whole fails to grasp the opportunity offered, we will publish the second edition of this book during the next shipping collapse in approximately twenty years' time.

In the event, I started to write chapter 1 of this second edition in the early spring of 1990, when despite my gloomy but subsequently justified prognostications the dry cargo market was enjoying the final peak of the bull market before its astonishing collapse in April, May and June. By now (mid-July) it is possible to look back over this sudden collapse and, avoiding the temptation either to wallow in the correctness of one's own market view or to carp on the short-sightedness of the shipping industry as a whole, to ask: "Has the shipping industry grasped the opportunity offered?" Have shipowners been protected from the worst effects of the recent fall by using freight futures? Has the shipping industry become more risk-conscious and more sophisticated in its approach to the management of the market risks which have always assailed it? The answer, I am afraid, is: Demonstrably not.

The volume traded on BIFFEX (and on the heavy fuel oil contracts) over the last five years are enough to prove that a very insignificant proportion of shipowners and merchants are so far using futures. And if the dry cargo market falls further over the next twelve months or so—perhaps back to the levels experienced in 1986—a significant contraction in the industry, together with the bankruptcies, redundancies and misery which that will entail, will be the result. And failure properly to have developed the freight futures market will have been a contributory factor in that misery.

The industry has demonstrably not so far used freight futures, and some of the damage which it seems destined now to suffer is the result.

But to be more constructive, let us examine for a moment why freight futures have not been more successful? As with most things, there seems to be a complex of reasons:

(1) The chicken and egg effect of the industry not being able to use a market until it is fully liquid, but it will never become liquid until more people are using it. This problem afflicts all new futures markets, and is not dissimilar in some respects to the "take-off point" lamentably never achieved by the Liberal vote.
(2) Lack of effort and liquidity-production by the futures brokers resulting from the way in which the market has been organised. It is becoming increasingly clear that a pit-traded system involving locals stands a much better chance of producing volume and liquidity than the rather old-fashioned ring trading approach of the Baltic. The BIFFEX and BFE authorities, it is true, have put a huge effort into marketing the concept, but they have never been able to produce a trading environment within which it could flourish.
(3) Problems with the contract: An index will always be a general reflection of the market. It is therefore impossible to take out a particular hedge with any degree of accuracy. Eventually the industry will come to accept the index as an instantly-recognisable yardstick, but until then they will always have difficulty identifying with it. Coupled with that general criticism have been a number of doubts about the construction of the index (e.g. whether or not time charter routes should be included) and about the method of its production. Most of these difficulties seem now to have been largely corrected, or the industry's perceptions and misconceptions changed, and the BFI now seems to be an industry-wide accepted yardstick of the dry-cargo market.
(4) The shipowner's reluctance to become a risk-manager. Most shipowners still seem to think they can make a decent living out of the asset-play side of shipowning. This means both that they are constitutionally reluctant to accept the possibility of a declining market and that they do not view a reduction in freight rates as being necessarily harmful. In short, shipowners are risk-hungry as well as risk-prone, and the removal of risk using futures is of no interest to them. A funny attitude, you may well think, but nonetheless the prevalent one.
(5) The reluctance of charterers other than the large grain houses, and the largest of freight operators, to become involved with BIFFEX. It is remarkable how few coal, ore and sugar interests are regular users of freight futures. This is probably mainly a problem of lack of education. The grain houses were always fully familiar with futures because of their age-old use of grain futures. It takes longer to educate other futures-illiterate cargo interests.

For all of this complex of reasons the shipping industry's usage of futures—freight futures, oil futures and financial futures—is still fairly limited. Whether the increasing degree of acceptance of the BFI, increasing financial sophistication of the main players, suitable structural and managerial changes in the futures industry, and above all a gradually changing attitude to risk-management among the shipowning community will be sufficient to change the overall usage of futures, only time will tell.

If the shipping industry fails to reform its attitude to risk management, if the futures industry fails to rise to the challenge of giving shipping a viable and active risk-management medium, the next cyclical collapse in the market will be as damaging as that in the mid-eighties.

The futures industry seems set to expand dramatically in a large number of different ways over the next five to ten years. An increasing variety of businesses will start to use futures and options, as new products are developed and the sophisticated usage of derivatives becomes increasingly commonplace. The futures and options markets are set to be even more exciting and dynamic in the 'nineties than they were in the 'eighties. It is my fervent hope that the shipping industry will be among those to benefit from these developments.

APPENDICES

APPENDIX I

FURTHER READING

James Gray: *Financial Risk Management in the Shipping Industry* (Fairplay, 1986).

Futures and Options for Shipping (Lloyd's of London Press, 1987).

Michael J. Hampton: *Long and Short Shipping Cycles* (Cambridge Academy of Transport, 1989).

Paul J. Veldhuizen: *Freight Futures : Targeting the 90's* (Lloyd's of London Press, 1989).

UNPUBLISHED UNIVERSITY THESES

"Freight Futures: A Review of its Development and Application in the Dry-Bulk Shipping Industry" (Paul J. Veldhuizen, Plymouth Polytechnic, 1987).

"The Future of Freight Futures" (Mark Solon, City University Business School, 1989).

"Ocean Freight Rate Futures Trading: An Economic Appraisal" (Alon Caspi, Noam Aurbach, University of Jerusalem, 1987).

"The Application of Modern Portfolio Theory to Hedging in Dry Bulk Shipping Markets" (Kevin Cullinane, Plymouth Polytechnic, 1989).

"Tanker Freight Futures" (Joong Ho Song, Plymouth Polytechnic, 1989).

APPENDIX II

THE BALTIC FREIGHT INDEX

A. HOW THE BALTIC FREIGHT INDEX (BFI) IS COMPUTED

A committee appointed by the Baltic Exchange has produced and keeps up to date a list of dry cargo freight routes. The committee is composed of leading London shipbrokers and is given the task of constantly reviewing the "constituent routes" to make sure that together they contribute a good representation of the dry cargo market and that they keep in line with the custom of the trade.

A panel of eight London-based shipbroking companies returns a rate on each of these routes to the Baltic Exchange, usually by 11a.m. The rate which they return will either be an actual fixture, if one has been reported that day, failing which it will be their expert view of what the rate would have been on that day if a fixture had been concluded. Their method of arriving at their daily list of rates is monitored by an independent auditor appointed by the Baltic Exchange.

By this means, the Baltic daily receives a list of eight rates on each of the routes. After a check for obvious errors, the top and the bottom rates are discarded and the remaining six are averaged. The Baltic thereby ends up with the average view of the rate on the particular route of eight of the largest and most professional shipbrokers in the world. The rest of the procedure is purely arithmetic and occurs in the Baltic's computer.

Each route is allocated a percentage weighting dependent on its perceived importance in the index as a whole and originally calculated from the relative importance of the route in tonne/mile terms in the world's dry cargo business.

For example, on "inception day", 4 January 1985, route 1,

Gulf/Holland grain, had a 20% weighting (since reduced to 10%). The index was set at 1,000 on that day. This meant that the average rate returned by the panellists had to be adjusted by a weighting factor, so that the contribution of that route would equal the percentage set. The average rate returned by the panellists on route 1 on 4/1/85 was US$9.078571. The weighting factor applied was therefore 22.029897717 to bring that figure to the 200 required (20% of 1,000). After 4/1/85, the average rate varies from day to day but the weighting factor remains constant to produce a change in the BFI. The average rates and weighting factors on the 14 routes are as follows:

Weighting factors for the component routes of the Baltic freight index

Route	Weighting(%)	Route Weighting Factor
1	10%	11.014948859
1a	10%	0.015263074
2	2%	13.999999999
3	7.5%	8.129451842
3a	7.5%	0.011157536
4	5%	4.283965728
5	5%	0.006497228
6	7.5%	7.106932105
7	5%	8.652657601
8	5%	4.416403785
9	5%	3.804347826
10	5%	11.111111111
11	2.5%	0.888404744
12	5%	3.343546262
	100%	

B. DAILY ROUTE INDICES

In addition to the main index, the Baltic Freight Index, or BFI, the method of calculation of which is described above in section A, the Baltic Exchange also produces every day a series of "Daily Route Indices".

These are indices on each individual route which were set, like the main index, on 4 January 1985, at 1000. They vary up and down thereafter in proportion to the relative strength or weakness of the route in question compared to the index as a whole.

Thus, if on a given day the BFI stood at 1500, but an individual route index stood at, for example, 2000, it would be reasonable to assume that the market for this route was disproportionately strong compared to the other routes.

These individual route indices can be used to improve the effectiveness and accuracy of a particular hedge, and are also useful in the computer plotting of the index against particular routes. Individual route indices are produced by multiplying the rate on that particular route by an individual route index factor. This factor will always remain constant, so that daily fluctuations in the route will be reflected in a fluctuating individual route index. The current individual route index factors are as follows:

Weighting factors for the component routes of the Baltic Freight Index—to show new route weighting factors as from Monday 6 August 1990 for Routes 1 and 3 and new routes 1A, 3A and 5

Route	Route Weighting Factor	Route Index Factor
1	11.014948859	110.149488586
1a	0.015263074	0.152623814
2	13.999999999	69.999999998
3	8.129451842	108.392691232
3a	0.011157536	0.148724832
4	4.283965728	85.679314568
5	0.006497228	0.123687606
6	7.106932105	96.952908589
7	8.652657601	173.053152026
8	4.416403785	88.328075713
9	3.804347826	76.086956520
10	11.111111111	222.222222222
11	0.888404744	28.011204482
12	3.343546262	73.839662446

APPENDIX II

C : QUICK CALCULATION OF INDEX EXPECTATIONS

It may from time to time be useful to know the effect which a particular change in a particular route would have on the index as a whole. A 10 cent change in the voyage routes, or $100 change in the time charter routes, would have approximately the following effect on the index:

Route	
1	1.10
1a	1.53
2	1.40
3	0.81
3a	1.12
4	0.43
5	0.65
6	0.71
7	0.87
8	0.44
9	0.38
10	1.11
11	0.09
12	0.33

APPENDIX III

THE BFI CONSTITUENT ROUTES: CURRENT AND HISTORICAL

The Baltic Exchange may alter the constituent routes to keep the index up to date within certain carefully calculated parameters. (Only a certain number of routes with a given percentage importance in the final calculation of the index may be changed in any one calendar year.) The exact rules under which the index is calculated and by which the routes may be changed are available on request from the Baltic Futures Exchange. (Patrick Neave, BFE 24–28 St Mary Axe, London EC3.) The full specification of the current routes effective 6/8/90 is as follows:

		Nominal Weightings
1.	1 Port US Gulf/Antwerp, Rotterdam, Amsterdam 55,000 Long tons 10 per cent light grain stowing 55 ft, free in and out. 10 days Sundays holidays excepted. Laydays 10 days forward from date of index, cancelling maximum 30 days forward from date of index. 3.75 per cent total commissions.	10%
1.A	Basis A standard 64,000 deadweight Hitachi type not aged over 15 years with a minimum of 2.6 millon cu.ft. grain, capable of about 13 on about 30 HVF + 2.5 diesel, for a Trans-Atlantic round of 45/60 days on the basis of delivery and redelivery Skaw Passero range. Cargo basis grain, ore or coal, or similar. 3.75 per cent total commissions.	10%
2.	1 port US Gulf/1 Combo Port South Japan 52,000 long tons 5 per cent heavy soya sorghum, free in and out, 11 days Sundays holidays excepted. Laydays 10 days forward from date of index, cancelling maximum 30 days forward from date of index. 3.75 per cent total commissions.	20%
3.	1 Port United States North Pacific/1 Combo Port South Japan, 52,000 long tons 5 per cent heavy soya sorghum, free in and out 11 days Sundays holidays excepted. Laydays 10 days forward from date of index, cancelling maximum 30 days forward from date of index. 3.75 per cent total commissions.	7.5%
3.A.	Basis A standard 64,000 deadweight Hitachi type not aged over 15 years with a minimum of 2.6 million cu.ft. grain, capable of about 13	

APPENDIX III

	on about 30 HVD + 2.5 diesel, for a Trans-Pacific round of 35/50 days either via Australia or Pacific (but not including short rounds such as Vostochny/Japan), delivery and redelivery Japan/South Korea range. Cargo basis grain, ore or coal, or similar. 3.75 per cent total commissions.	7.5%
4.	1 port US Gulf/Venezuela 21,000 metric tonnes 5 per cent heavy soya sorgum 4 days/1,000 free in and out. Laydays 10 days forward from date of index. Cancelling 25 days forward from date of index. 3.75 per cent total commissions.	5%
5.	Basis A vessel not aged over 15 years in size range 38,000/42,000 about 14 knots on 30 HVF + 2 diesel, basis delivery Skaw Passero range, for a trip via East Coast S. America to the Far East, redelivery Singapore/Japan Inc. China, duration 60/80 days, 25 ton crane, cargo basis steel. 3.75 per cent total commissions.	5%
6.	1 Port Hampton Roads and Richards Bay or 1 Port Hampton Roads only/1 Port South Japan 120,000 long tons 10 per cent coal free in and out and trimmed 8 days Sundays holidays included. 15,000 Richards Bay, laydays 10 days forward from date of index, cancelling maximum 30 days forward from date of index. 3.75 per cent total commissions.	7.5%
7.	1 Port Hampton Roads excluding Baltimore/1 Port Antwerp, Rotterdam, Amsterdam, 65,000 metric tonnes 10 per cent coal, free in and out and trimmed 5 days Sundays holidays included/Sundays holidays excepted. Laydays 10 days forward from date of index, cancelling maximum 30 days forward from date of index. 3.75 per cent total commissions.	5%
8.	Queensland/Rotterdam 110,000 long tons 10 per cent coal, free in and out 40,000 Sundays holidays included/25,000 Sundays holidays excepted. Laydays 15 days forward from date of index, cancelling 25 days forward from date of index. 5 per cent total commissions.	5%
9.	Vancouver-San Diego range/Rotterdam 55,000 metric tonnes 10 per cent petroleum coke free in and out 10,000 Sundays holidays included 10,000 Sundays holidays excepted. Laydays 15 days forward from date of index, cancelling 25 days forward from date of index. 5 per cent total commissions.	5%
10.	Monrovia/Rotterdam 90,000 long tons 10 per cent iron ore, free in and out 5 days Sundays holidays included. Laydays 15 days forward from date of index, cancelling maximum 30 days forward from date of index. 3.75 per cent total commissions.	5%
11.	Casablanca/West Coast India (30ft SWAD) 15/25,000 metric tonnes phosphate rock scale gross/1,000 free laydays 10 days forward from date of index, cancelling 25 days forward from date of index. 5 per cent total commissions.	2.5%
12.	Aqaba/1 Port West Coast India 14,000 metric tonnes 5 per cent phosphate rock free in and out scale/1,000. Laydays 10 days forward from date of index, cancelling 25 days forward from date of index. 5 per cent total commissions.	5%
		100%

The following are the changes which have previously occurred in the index:

6 August 1990   Introduction of time charter routes

New routes

1a: Panamax Trans-Atlantic Route
3a: Trans-Pacific Route
New Route 5: Handimax del Skaw/Passero
Time charter trip to Far East. (Which replaces old route 5 Antwerp/ Jeddah 35,000, 10% bulk barley 4,000 SHEX/3,000 Shex Fio. Laydays 10 days forward from date of index, cancelling 25 days forward from date of index, 3.75% brokerage. 5% weighting.)

5 February 1990   Minor amendments to route definitions

4 November 1988   Amendment and introduction of new route

Route 6: Hampton Roads and Richards Bay/South Japan. Nominal weighting increased from 5% to 7.5%.
New route 11: Casablanca/West Coast India, replaces Victoria/China. Nominal weighting 2.5% (from 5%).
Route 12: Hamburg/West Coast India, removed.
Route 13: Aqaba/West Coast India, becomes route 12 with nominal weighting 5%.
Old Route 11: Vitoria/1 port China (31 FWAD), 25,000/10% Pig Iron, 3,000/2,000 Sinochart Terms Fio, laydays 15 days forward from date of index, cancelling 35 days forward from the date of index, 6.25% brokerage, 5% weighting.
Old Route 12: Hamburg/West Coast India, 13/20,000 Muriate of Potash, 3,500/1,000 Fio, laydays 10 days forward from date of index, cancelling 25 days forward from date of index, 5% brokerage, 2.5% weighting.

8 May 1986

New Route 11: Vitoria/China, which replaces Very Old Route 11, Recife/US East Coast.
Very Old Route 11: Recife/US East Coast, 20,000 5% Bulk sugar, 750 mechanical/1500 FIOT, laydays 10 days forward from date of index, cancelling 30 days forward from date of index, 6.25% brokerage, 5% weighting.

APPENDIX III

6 February 1986

New Route 5: Antwerp/Jeddah which replaces Very Old Route 5, Antwerp/1 Port Red Sea.

Very Old Route 5: Antwerp/Red Sea, 20,000/5% Bagged Barley 2,500/1,000 Fio, laydays 10 days forward from date of index, cancelling 25 days forward from date of index. 5% brokerage, 5% weighting.

For comparison purposes, the following is the list of routes introduced on 5 January 1985.

		Weighting %
1.	1 port US Gulf/Antwerp, Rotterdam, Amsterdam 55,000 5%, Heavy Soya Sorgum, free in and out. 11 days Sundays holidays excepted, laydays 10 days forward from date of index, cancelling maximum 30 days forward from date of index 3.75% brokerage.	20
2.	1 Port US Gulf/1 port South Japan 52,000 5% Heavy Soya Sorgum free in and out 11 days Sundays holidays excepted, laydays 10 days forward from date of index, cancelling maximum 30 days forward from date of index 3.75% brokerage.	20
3.	1 port United States North Pacific/1 port South Japan 52,000 5% Heavy Soya Sorghum free in and out 11 days Sundays holidays excepted, laydays 10 days forward from date of index, cancelling maximum 30 days forward from date of index 3.75% brokerage.	15
4.	1 port US Gulf/Venezuela 21,000 5% Heavy Soya Sorgum 4 days/1,000 free in and out laydays 10 forward from date of index, cancelling 25 days forward from date of index, 3.75% brokerage.	5
5.	Antwerp/1 port Red Sea 20,000 5% Bagged Barley free in and out 2,500/1,000 laydays 10 days forward from date of index, cancelling 25 days forward from date of index, 5% brokerage.	5
6.	1 Port Hampton Roads and Richards Bay/1 port South Japan 120,000 10% Coal 8 days Sundays holidays included, 15,000 Richards Bay, laydays 10 days forward from date of index, cancelling maximum 30 days from date of index, 3.75 brokerage.	5
7.	1 port Hampton Roads excluding Baltimore/1 port Antwerp Rotterdam Amsterdam 65,000 10% Coal 5 days Sundays holidays included/Sundays holidays	

BFI CONSTITUENT ROUTES

	excepted, laydays 10 days forward from date of index, cancelling maximum 30 days from date of index, 3.75% brokerage.	5
8.	Queensland/Rotterdam 110,000/10% Coal free in and out 40,000 Sundays holidays included/25,000 Sundays holidays excepted, laydays 15 days forward from date of index, cancelling 25 days forward from date of index, 5% brokerage.	5
9.	Vancouver-San Diego Range/Rotterdam 55,000/10% Petroleum Coke free in and out 10,000 Sundays holidays included/10,000 Sundays holidays excepted, laydays 15 days forward from date of index, cancelling maximum 25 days forward from date of index, 3.75% brokerage.	5
10.	Monrovia/Rotterdam 90,000 10% Iron Ore, 5 days Sundays holidays included, laydays 15 days forward from date of index, cancelling maximum 30 days forward from date of index, 3.75% brokerage.	
11.	Recife/1 port United States East Coast 20,000 5% Bulk Sugar free in and out and trimmed 750 mechanical/1,500, laydays 10 days forward from date of index, cancelling maximum 30 days from date of index, 6.25% brokerage.	5
12.	Hamburg/West Coast India 13/20,000 Muriate of Potash free in and out 3,500/1,000 laydays 10 days forward from date of index, cancelling 25 days forward for date of index, 5% brokerage.	2.5
13.	Aqaba/1 port West Coast India 14,000 5% Phosphate Rock free in and out 3,500/1,000 laydays 10 days forward from date of index, cancelling 25 days forward from date of index, 5% brokerage.	2.5

APPENDIX IV

BALTIC FREIGHT INDEX SINCE 4.1.85

January 85		March 85		May 85	
4th	1000.0	1st	984.0	1st	1062.0
7th	998.5	4th	982.5	2nd	1058.5
8th	996.5	5th	979.5	3rd	1058.0
9th	994.5	6th	987.0	7th	1056.5
10th	979.5	7th	990.0	8th	1056.0
11th	980.5	8th	988.5	9th	1053.0
14th	974.0	11th	991.5	10th	1032.0
15th	973.0	12th	990.5	13th	1024.0
16th	979.0	13th	991.5	14th	1018.0
17th	984.0	14th	990.5	15th	1009.5
18th	983.5	15th	994.0	16th	999.5
21st	975.5	18th	999.5	17th	990.5
22nd	975.5	19th	1002.0	20th	989.5
23rd	977.0	20th	999.5	21st	984.0
24th	975.0	21st	1000.5	22nd	979.0
25th	971.5	22nd	997.5	23rd	974.5
28th	970.5	25th	996.5	24th	968.0
29th	972.5	26th	997.5	28th	954.5
30th	973.0	27th	997.0	29th	950.0
31st	971.5	28th	1008.5	30th	942.0
		29th	1016.5	31st	931.5
February 85		April 85		June 85	
1st	973.5	1st	1018.5	3rd	931.0
4th	973.5	2nd	1020.0	4th	929.5
5th	971.5	3rd	1025.5	5th	931.0
6th	969.5	4th	1026.0	6th	931.5
7th	969.0	9th	1022.0	7th	930.5
8th	966.5	10th	1022.5	10th	926.0
11th	967.0	11th	1023.5	11th	922.5
12th	966.0	12th	1027.5	12th	919.0
13th	965.5	15th	1064.5	13th	917.0
14th	966.5	16th	1064.0	14th	926.0
15th	973.5	17th	1057.5	17th	927.5
18th	973.0	18th	1056.0	18th	925.0
19th	971.5	19th	1059.0	19th	918.0
20th	973.5	22nd	1062.0	20th	911.0
21st	976.5	23rd	1062.0	21st	896.0
22nd	983.5	24th	1058.5	24th	892.5
25th	985.0	25th	1057.5	25th	891.0
26th	986.0	26th	1057.0	26th	890.0
27th	986.5	29th	1059.0	27th	883.5
28th	984.0	30th	1063.0	28th	872.5

APPENDIX IV

July 85
1st	864.5
2nd	854.0
3rd	838.0
4th	817.5
5th	807.0
8th	803.0
9th	801.0
10th	792.5
11th	791.5
12th	784.5
15th	775.5
16th	773.0
17th	769.5
18th	763.5
19th	763.5
22nd	760.5
23rd	759.5
24th	754.5
25th	748.5
26th	746.0
29th	732.0
30th	728.5
31st	725.5

August 85
1st	718.5
2nd	716.5
5th	716.0
6th	714.5
7th	711.5
8th	713.0
9th	716.5
12th	717.0
13th	717.5
14th	718.5
15th	724.0
16th	726.0
19th	725.5
20th	729.5
21st	731.5
22nd	736.0
23rd	740.5
27th	741.5
28th	740.5
29th	739.0
30th	738.0

September 85
2nd	738.5
3rd	739.5
4th	739.5
5th	737.0
6th	735.0
9th	736.5
10th	740.0
11th	747.0
12th	755.0
13th	759.5
16th	759.5
17th	760.5
18th	765.0
19th	779.0
20th	805.5
23rd	820.5
24th	826.0
25th	839.5
26th	866.5
27th	883.0
30th	893.5

October 85
1st	905.5
2nd	906.0
3rd	903.0
4th	886.5
7th	884.0
8th	883.0
9th	868.5
10th	869.0
11th	872.5
14th	883.5
15th	888.5
16th	888.5
17th	891.0
18th	895.5
21st	897.0
22nd	898.0
23rd	898.5
24th	903.0
25th	902.5
28th	902.0
29th	902.5
30th	904.0
31st	905.0

November 85
1st	906.5
4th	910.0
5th	913.5
6th	914.5
7th	911.0
8th	910.0
11th	898.5
12th	894.5
13th	891.5
14th	891.0
15th	890.5
18th	892.0
19th	895.0
20th	903.5
21st	903.0
22nd	902.5
25th	901.5
26th	901.0
27th	900.0
28th	912.5
29th	915.0

December 85
2nd	916.0
3rd	919.5
4th	920.0
5th	921.5
6th	920.5
9th	918.5
10th	917.5
11th	916.0
12th	910.0
13th	907.0
16th	902.5
17th	900.0
18th	897.0
19th	895.0
20th	893.5
23rd	893.5
24th	894.0
30th	895.5
31st	898.0

January 86
2nd	897.5
3rd	897.5
6th	904.0
7th	902.5
8th	905.5
9th	914.5
10th	919.5
13th	917.5
14th	917.0
15th	912.5
16th	909.0
18th	906.5
20th	907.5
21st	904.0
22nd	894.0
23rd	892.0
24th	887.0
27th	883.0
28th	869.0
29th	846.0
30th	836.5
31st	831.0

February 86
3rd	827.5
4th	821.0
5th	811.5
6th	799.0
7th	796.0
10th	796.0
11th	789.0

BFI SINCE 1985

12th	786.5	30th	658.5	14th	571.5
13th	784.0			15th	570.5
14th	780.0	**May 86**		16th	572.5
17th	770.5	1st	658.0	17th	574.5
18th	768.0	2nd	654.5	18th	574.0
19th	761.0	6th	654.5	21st	572.0
20th	753.0	7th	653.5	22nd	570.5
21st	749.0	8th	654.5	23rd	569.0
24th	742.0	9th	656.5	24th	567.5
25th	739.0	12th	659.0	25th	566.5
26th	737.5	13th	658.5	28th	567.0
27th	737.0	14th	661.0	29th	559.0
28th	737.0	15th	669.0	30th	556.5
		16th	668.0	31st	553.5
March 86		19th	664.0		
3rd	734.0	20th	664.5	**August 86**	
4th	733.0	21st	665.0	1st	556.0
5th	736.0	22nd	664.5	4th	554.0
6th	739.0	23rd	664.0	5th	554.0
7th	739.0	27th	662.5	6th	554.5
10th	741.0	28th	664.0	7th	555.0
11th	742.0	29th	665.0	8th	556.5
12th	742.5	30th	665.0	11th	558.5
13th	745.5			12th	562.0
14th	743.5	**June 86**		13th	568.0
17th	744.0	2nd	663.0	14th	570.5
18th	746.5	3rd	662.5	15th	572.5
19th	748.0	4th	661.5	18th	574.0
20th	746.5	5th	661.0	19th	576.5
21st	744.5	6th	664.0	20th	589.0
24th	742.5	9th	665.0	21st	607.5
25th	739.5	10th	664.0	22nd	628.0
26th	736.5	11th	659.5	26th	636.0
27th	733.5	12th	658.0	27th	644.5
		13th	654.0	28th	658.5
April 86		16th	650.5	29th	664.0
1st	732.5	17th	650.0		
2nd	731.5	18th	648.5	**September 86**	
3rd	731.0	19th	646.5	1st	672.0
4th	727.5	20th	639.0	2nd	678.5
7th	723.0	23rd	637.0	3rd	700.0
8th	713.5	24th	636.5	4th	714.5
9th	705.0	25th	620.5	5th	718.5
10th	701.5	26th	592.5	8th	728.0
11th	695.5	27th	586.5	9th	733.5
14th	689.0	30th	585.5	10th	735.5
15th	683.5			11th	743.0
16th	681.0	**July 86**		12th	750.5
17th	682.0	1st	584.5	15th	751.5
18th	685.0	2nd	585.0	16th	753.0
21st	685.5	3rd	582.5	17th	756.0
22nd	680.5	4th	582.0	18th	763.5
23rd	676.0	7th	581.0	19th	770.5
24th	674.0	8th	581.0	22nd	773.5
25th	667.0	9th	579.0	23rd	770.5
28th	664.0	10th	576.5	24th	771.5
29th	659.0	11th	572.5	25th	789.5

APPENDIX IV

26th	792.5	8th	710.0	25th	848.5
29th	800.0	9th	709.0	26th	851.0
30th	799.5	10th	708.0	27th	852.5
		11th	706.5		
October 86		12th	705.5	**March 87**	
1st	794.5	15th	706.0	2nd	856.5
2nd	795.5	16th	705.0	3rd	859.0
3rd	795.0	17th	700.5	4th	859.5
6th	794.0	18th	699.0	5th	861.5
7th	794.0	19th	696.0	6th	865.5
8th	795.0	22nd	694.5	9th	868.5
9th	792.5	23rd	694.0	10th	871.5
10th	791.5	24th	693.5	11th	873.0
13th	788.0	29th	696.0	12th	883.5
14th	788.5	30th	697.0	13th	889.5
15th	786.5	31st	699.0	16th	903.5
16th	793.5			17th	907.0
17th	794.0	**January 87**		18th	909.0
20th	789.0	5th	703.0	19th	924.0
21st	784.0	6th	710.5	20th	946.5
22nd	786.0	7th	719.5	23rd	953.5
23rd	786.0	8th	739.5	24th	959.0
24th	784.5	9th	765.5	25th	980.0
27th	786.0	12th	788.5	26th	988.0
28th	785.5	13th	789.0	27th	991.5
29th	786.5	14th	803.0	30th	991.0
30th	786.0	15th	813.5	31st	991.5
31st	786.5	16th	827.0		
		19th	852.5	**April 87**	
November 86		20th	857.5	1st	998.0
3rd	784.0	21st	853.5	2nd	1014.0
4th	781.5	22nd	853.0	3rd	1025.0
5th	779.0	23rd	863.0	6th	1033.0
6th	777.0	26th	863.5	7th	1030.5
7th	780.0	27th	863.0	8th	1023.5
10th	787.0	28th	863.5	9th	1023.0
11th	785.5	29th	866.5	10th	1018.0
12th	781.0	30th	866.5	13th	1010.5
13th	779.5			14th	1007.5
14th	779.0	**February 87**		15th	1001.0
17th	778.0	2nd	861.5	16th	999.5
18th	777.5	3rd	858.5	21st	1000.5
19th	774.5	4th	856.5	22nd	1002.5
20th	770.5	5th	855.5	23rd	1003.0
21st	766.0	6th	855.0	24th	1006.5
24th	762.5	9th	855.5	27th	1013.5
25th	757.5	10th	855.0	28th	1016.0
26th	749.5	11th	853.5	29th	1019.0
27th	747.0	12th	856.0	30th	1019.5
28th	737.5	13th	855.0		
		16th	855.0	**May 87**	
December 86		17th	853.5	1st	1025.0
1st	736.0	18th	855.5	5th	1027.0
2nd	730.5	19th	851.0	6th	1034.0
3rd	721.5	20th	850.0	7th	1051.5
4th	718.0	23rd	851.5	8th	1065.5
5th	713.0	24th	848.0	11th	1077.5

12th	1083.5	28th	973.0	7th	1075.0
13th	1087.5	29th	965.0	8th	1079.5
14th	1102.0	30th	969.5	9th	1084.0
15th	1101.0	31st	976.5	12th	1085.5
18th	1100.0			13th	1086.5
19th	1094.0	**August 87**		14th	1085.5
20th	1087.5	3rd	982.5	15th	1088.5
21st	1084.5	4th	993.5	16th	1088.5
22nd	1083.5	5th	1003.0	19th	1097.5
26th	1079.0	6th	1014.5	20th	1105.0
27th	1075.0	7th	1039.0	21st	1123.5
28th	1076.0	10th	1060.0	22nd	1136.0
29th	1070.5	11th	1074.0	23rd	1144.5
		12th	1118.5	26th	1148.0
June 87		13th	1125.5	27th	1148.0
1st	1069.5	14th	1127.0	28th	1158.0
2nd	1047.0	17th	1129.0	29th	1168.5
3rd	1024.5	18th	1128.5	30th	1171.5
4th	1015.0	19th	1129.0		
5th	989.5	20th	1129.0	**November 87**	
8th	986.5	21st	1128.0	2nd	1172.5
9th	985.5	24th	1127.5	3rd	1172.0
10th	980.5	25th	1119.5	4th	1171.5
11th	977.0	26th	1102.0	5th	1174.0
12th	977.0	27th	1110.5	6th	1175.0
15th	973.5	28th	1111.0	9th	1175.0
16th	966.0			10th	1173.5
17th	960.5	**September 87**		11th	1172.5
18th	948.5	1st	1105.0	12th	1170.5
19th	938.0	2nd	1084.5	13th	1163.5
22nd	929.0	3rd	1066.0	16th	1155.5
23rd	925.0	4th	1063.5	17th	1154.0
24th	917.0	7th	1060.5	18th	1155.5
25th	901.0	8th	1060.5	19th	1153.0
26th	891.5	9th	1061.5	20th	1152.0
29th	886.0	10th	1061.5	23rd	1153.5
30th	879.5	11th	1060.5	24th	1159.0
		14th	1049.0	25th	1168.0
July 87		15th	1048.0	26th	1169.0
1st	874.0	16th	1046.0	27th	1171.5
2nd	874.5	17th	1038.0	30th	1175.5
3rd	883.5	18th	1034.0		
6th	893.0	21st	1031.5	**December 87**	
7th	911.0	22nd	1035.0	1st	1183.5
8th	919.5	23rd	1026.0	2nd	1213.5
9th	923.0	24th	1033.0	3rd	1226.5
10th	923.5	25th	1038.5	4th	1231.0
13th	922.0	28th	1043.0	7th	1238.0
14th	921.5	29th	1043.0	8th	1259.0
15th	923.5	30th	1045.0	9th	1270.0
16th	924.5	31st	1052.0	10th	1267.0
17th	930.0			11th	1269.5
20th	948.0	**October 87**		14th	1271.0
21st	955.5	1st	1052.0	15th	1268.5
22nd	966.5	2nd	1063.5	16th	1268.0
23rd	969.5	5th	1067.5	17th	1264.5
24th	972.5	6th	1071.0	18th	1259.5
27th	974.5				

21st	1260.0	4th	1569.5	23rd	1419.5
22nd	1261.5	7th	1570.0	24th	1414.5
23rd	1262.0	8th	1571.0	25th	1404.0
24th	1262.5	9th	1575.0	26th	1392.0
29th	1261.5	10th	1576.5	27th	1370.0
30th	1259.0	11th	1582.0	31st	1349.0
31st	1263.5	14th	1583.5		
		15th	1590.0	**June 88**	
January 88		16th	1596.5	1st	1328.5
4th	1265.5	17th	1610.5	2nd	1320.0
5th	1270.0	18th	1630.0	3rd	1303.5
6th	1284.5	21st	1640.0	6th	1295.5
7th	1295.5	22nd	1647.5	7th	1288.0
8th	1319.5	23rd	1648.5	8th	1287.0
11th	1350.0	24th	1645.5	9th	1283.5
12th	1361.5	25th	1645.0	10th	1284.5
13th	1368.0	28th	1641.5	13th	1283.5
14th	1374.5	29th	1630.0	14th	1279.0
15th	1384.0	30th	1621.5	15th	1276.0
18th	1386.5	31st	1617.0	16th	1262.0
19th	1390.5			17th	1258.5
20th	1398.0	**April 88**		20th	1254.0
21st	1402.5	5th	1612.0	21st	1249.0
22nd	1400.0	6th	1596.5	22nd	1244.5
25th	1394.0	7th	1588.0	23rd	1242.0
26th	1391.0	8th	1584.0	24th	1242.0
27th	1390.0	11th	1571.5	27th	1238.5
28th	1387.5	12th	1560.5	28th	1231.5
29th	1393.0	13th	1544.0	29th	1224.0
		14th	1541.5	30th	1208.5
February 88		15th	1527.5		
1st	1399.5	18th	1519.0	**July 88**	
2nd	1408.5	19th	1493.0	1st	1206.0
3rd	1427.0	20th	1475.0	4th	1206.0
4th	1468.5	21st	1441.5	5th	1210.0
5th	1488.0	22nd	1415.5	6th	1200.0
8th	1499.5	25th	1402.5	7th	1186.0
9th	1514.0	26th	1393.5	8th	1186.0
10th	1516.0	27th	1377.5	11th	1183.0
11th	1534.0	28th	1368.5	12th	1183.0
12th	1547.0	29th	1358.0	13th	1180.0
15th	1544.0			14th	1178.0
16th	1545.5	**May 88**		15th	1171.0
17th	1561.5	3rd	1345.0	18th	1178.0
18th	1566.0	4th	1339.0	19th	1189.0
19th	1568.5	5th	1344.0	20th	1199.0
22nd	1567.0	6th	1375.5	21st	1196.0
23rd	1563.5	9th	1387.0	22nd	1201.0
24th	1562.0	10th	1391.0	25th	1199.0
25th	1560.5	11th	1397.5	26th	1199.0
26th	1562.0	12th	1428.5	27th	1197.0
29th	1563.5	13th	1445.0	28th	1197.0
		16th	1446.0	29th	1197.0
March 88		17th	1452.0		
1st	1562.5	18th	1455.5	**August 88**	
2nd	1562.0	19th	1438.0	1st	1196.0
3rd	1564.0	20th	1420.0	2nd	1192.0

BFI SINCE 1985

3rd	1192.0	18th	1315.0	January 89	
4th	1191.0	19th	1317.0	3rd	1544.0
5th	1192.0	20th	1316.0	4th	1553.0
8th	1192.0	21st	1328.0	5th	1555.0
9th	1190.0	24th	1361.0	6th	1578.0
10th	1191.0	25th	1363.0	9th	1589.0
11th	1191.0	26th	1364.0	10th	1604.0
12th	1195.0	27th	1369.0	11th	1620.0
15th	1209.0	28th	1371.0	12th	1629.0
16th	1211.0	31st	1373.0	13th	1635.0
17th	1215.0			16th	1642.0
18th	1240.0	November 88		17th	1643.0
19th	1246.0	1st	1378.0	18th	1650.0
22nd	1244.0	2nd	1390.0	19th	1648.0
23rd	1248.0	3rd	1396.0	20th	1644.0
24th	1252.0	4th	1398.0	23rd	1646.0
25th	1253.0	7th	1410.0	24th	1645.0
26th	1261.0	8th	1415.0	25th	1634.0
30th	1267.0	9th	1420.0	26th	1633.0
31st	1272.0	10th	1424.0	27th	1617.0
		11th	1434.0	30th	1619.0
September 88		14th	1444.0	31st	1619.0
1st	1272.0	15th	1454.0		
2nd	1271.0	16th	1473.0	February 89	
5th	1278.0	17th	1482.0	1st	1608.0
6th	1279.0	18th	1492.0	2nd	1607.0
7th	1277.0	21st	1495.0	3rd	1584.0
8th	1283.0	22nd	1503.0	6th	1553.0
9th	1282.0	23rd	1517.0	7th	1542.0
12th	1278.0	24th	1517.0	8th	1533.0
13th	1283.0	25th	1512.0	9th	1526.0
14th	1284.0	28th	1511.0	10th	1523.0
15th	1283.0	29th	1510.0	13th	1511.0
16th	1289.0	30th	1501.0	14th	1506.0
19th	1289.0			15th	1503.0
20th	1288.0	December 88		16th	1499.0
21st	1285.0	1st	1501.0	17th	1495.0
22nd	1285.0	2nd	1490.0	20th	1502.0
23rd	1286.0	5th	1488.0	21st	1506.0
26th	1286.0	6th	1487.0	22nd	1512.0
27th	1289.0	7th	1485.0	23rd	1513.0
28th	1269.0	8th	1486.0	24th	1529.0
29th	1266.0	9th	1494.0	27th	1543.0
30th	1270.0	12th	1514.0	28th	1553.0
		13th	1518.0		
October 88		14th	1522.0	March 89	
3rd	1275.0	15th	1524.0	1st	1563.0
4th	1277.0	16th	1518.0	2nd	1577.0
5th	1283.0	19th	1517.0	3rd	1588.0
6th	1291.0	20th	1518.0	6th	1593.0
7th	1291.0	21st	1523.0	7th	1597.0
10th	1292.0	22nd	1523.0	8th	1608.0
11th	1294.0	23rd	1527.0	9th	1615.0
12th	1305.0	28th	1529.0	10th	1623.0
13th	1308.0	29th	1540.0	13th	1624.0
14th	1321.0	30th	1543.0	14th	1632.0
17th	1314.0			15th	1640.0

		June 89		14th	1405.0
16th	1647.0	1st	1587.0	15th	1409.0
17th	1645.0	2nd	1484.0	16th	1417.0
20th	1644.0	5th	1450.0	17th	1421.0
21st	1644.0	6th	1445.0	18th	1421.0
22nd	1640.0	7th	1425.0	21st	1421.0
23rd	1638.0	8th	1412.0	22nd	1423.0
28th	1632.0	9th	1406.0	23rd	1427.0
29th	1631.0	12th	1400.0	24th	1427.0
30th	1624.0	13th	1390.0	25th	1426.0
31st	1631.0	14th	1390.0	29th	1425.0
		15th	1396.0	30th	1425.0
April 89		16th	1397.0	31st	1426.0
3rd	1619.0	19th	1396.0		
4th	1614.0	20th	1396.0	September 89	
5th	1621.0	21st	1400.0	1st	1426.0
6th	1620.0	22nd	1407.0	4th	1428.0
7th	1622.0	23rd	1399.0	5th	1429.0
10th	1623.0	26th	1399.0	6th	1433.0
11th	1621.0	27th	1391.0	7th	1436.0
12th	1622.0	28th	1393.0	8th	1437.0
13th	1619.0	29th	1410.0	11th	1441.0
14th	1626.0	30th	1413.0	12th	1440.0
17th	1627.0			13th	1437.0
18th	1621.0	July 89		14th	1434.0
19th	1617.0	3rd	1414.0	15th	1433.0
20th	1620.0	4th	1413.0	18th	1434.0
21st	1617.0	5th	1401.0	19th	1439.0
24th	1619.0	6th	1398.0	20th	1435.0
25th	1621.0	7th	1392.0	21st	1425.0
26th	1622.0	10th	1391.0	22nd	1425.0
27th	1624.0	11th	1390.0	25th	1424.0
28th	1629.0	12th	1400.0	26th	1420.0
		13th	1401.0	27th	1413.0
May 89		14th	1392.0	28th	1421.0
2nd	1641.0	17th	1385.0	29th	1420.0
3rd	1649.0	18th	1380.0		
4th	1687.0	19th	1377.0	October 89	
5th	1693.0	20th	1376.0	2nd	1424.0
8th	1699.0	21st	1376.0	3rd	1436.0
9th	1704.0	24th	1379.0	4th	1451.0
10th	1715.0	25th	1379.0	5th	1459.0
11th	1727.0	26th	1388.0	6th	1469.0
12th	1748.0	27th	1388.0	9th	1470.0
15th	1749.0	28th	1389.0	10th	1476.0
16th	1751.0	31st	1397.0	11th	1479.0
17th	1744.0			12th	1486.0
18th	1748.0	August 89		13th	1494.0
19th	1744.0	1st	1392.0	16th	1509.0
22nd	1730.0	2nd	1390.0	17th	1516.0
23rd	1722.0	3rd	1390.0	18th	1545.0
24th	1712.0	4th	1387.0	19th	1554.0
25th	1682.0	7th	1379.0	20th	1593.0
26th	1667.0	8th	1381.0	23rd	1599.0
29th	1626.0	9th	1383.0	24th	1612.0
30th	1596.0	10th	1394.0	25th	1624.0
		11th	1401.0	26th	1627.0

27th	1636.0	11th	1655.0	27th	1546.0
30th	1641.0	12th	1658.0	28th	1539.0
31st	1647.0	15th	1660.0	29th	1532.0
		16th	1663.0	30th	1529.0
November 89		17th	1663.0		
1st	1647.0	18th	1664.0	**April 90**	
2nd	1651.0	19th	1669.0	2nd	1528.0
3rd	1653.0	22nd	1668.0	3rd	1513.0
6th	1654.0	23rd	1663.0	4th	1499.0
7th	1654.0	24th	1653.0	5th	1483.0
8th	1657.0	25th	1646.0	6th	1466.0
9th	1654.0	26th	1651.0	9th	1462.0
10th	1656.0	29th	1648.0	10th	1462.0
13th	1650.0	30th	1644.0	11th	1459.0
14th	1648.0	31st	1644.0	12th	1456.0
15th	1648.0			17th	1447.0
16th	1648.0	**February 90**		18th	1444.0
17th	1652.0	1st	1642.0	19th	1436.0
20th	1656.0	2nd	1638.0	20th	1418.0
21st	1670.0	5th	1619.0	23rd	1414.0
22nd	1668.0	6th	1606.0	24th	1402.0
23rd	1670.0	7th	1588.0	25th	1390.0
24th	1672.0	8th	1583.0	26th	1379.0
27th	1673.0	9th	1583.0	27th	1373.0
28th	1671.0	12th	1579.0	30th	1361.0
29th	1666.0	13th	1579.0		
30th	1653.0	14th	1578.0	**May 90**	
		15th	1576.0	1st	1355.0
December 89		16th	1576.0	2nd	1352.0
1st	1640.0	19th	1576.0	3rd	1345.0
4th	1629.0	20th	1592.0	4th	1340.0
5th	1610.0	21st	1591.0	8th	1330.0
6th	1606.0	22nd	1591.0	9th	1321.0
7th	1605.0	23rd	1591.0	10th	1317.0
8th	1605.0	26th	1593.0	11th	1313.0
11th	1603.0	27th	1603.0	14th	1305.0
12th	1604.0	28th	1604.0	15th	1305.0
13th	1603.0			16th	1305.0
14th	1602.0	**March 90**		17th	1309.0
15th	1603.0	1st	1603.0	18th	1311.0
18th	1603.0	2nd	1606.0	21st	1315.0
19th	1596.0	5th	1610.0	22nd	1316.0
20th	1592.0	6th	1614.0	23rd	1317.0
21st	1590.0	7th	1618.0	24th	1317.0
22nd	1586.0	8th	1622.0	25th	1313.0
27th	1585.0	9th	1629.0	29th	1304.0
28th	1584.0	12th	1628.0	30th	1303.0
29th	1592.0	13th	1628.0	31st	1299.0
		14th	1627.0		
January 90		15th	1620.0	**June 90**	
2nd	1599.0	16th	1606.0	1st	1301.0
3rd	1602.0	19th	1594.0	4th	1302.0
4th	1609.0	20th	1590.0	5th	1305.0
5th	1619.0	21st	1570.0	6th	1302.0
8th	1637.0	22nd	1569.0	7th	1297.0
9th	1644.0	23rd	1557.0	8th	1275.0
10th	1652.0	26th	1550.0	11th	1264.0

12th	1254.0	20th	1129.0
13th	1243.0	23rd	1135.0
14th	1232.0	24th	1141.0
15th	1219.0	25th	1142.0
18th	1197.0	26th	1150.0
19th	1181.0	27th	1157.0
20th	1169.0	30th	1161.0
21st	1159.0	31st	1165.0
22nd	1152.0		
25th	1148.0	**August 90**	
26th	1144.0	1st	1175.0
27th	1128.0	2nd	1185.0
28th	1110.0	3rd	1180.0
29th	1089.0	6th	1182.0
		7th	1188.0
July 90		8th	1206.0
2nd	1082.0	9th	1220.0
3rd	1075.0	10th	1232.0
4th	1073.0	13th	1237.0
5th	1065.0	14th	1237.0
6th	1067.0	15th	1236.0
9th	1068.0	16th	1228.0
10th	1069.0	17th	1226.0
11th	1056.0	20th	1222.0
12th	1064.0	21st	1222.0
13th	1075.0	22nd	1220.0
16th	1080.0	23rd	1221.0
17th	1086.0	24th	1220.0
18th	1091.0	27th	1215.0
19th	1095.0	28th	1210.0

APPENDIX V

TABLE OF BIFFEX CONTRACT AVAILABILITY

The following chart indicates the months available on BIFFEX. The months underlined are the new months introduced on that particular date.

Contracts available

Date	*Spot*	*Prompt*	*Quarterlies*
1 Jan	Jan	<u>Feb</u>	Apr, Jul, Oct, Jan, Apr, Jul, Oct
1 Feb	Feb	<u>Mar</u>	Apr, Jul, Oct, Jan, Apr, Jul, Oct, <u>Jan</u>
1 Mar	Mar	Apr	Jul, Oct, Jan, Apr, Jul, Oct, Jan
1 Apr	Apr	<u>May</u>	Jul, Oct, Jan, Apr, Jul, Oct, Jan
1 May	May	<u>Jun</u>	Jul, Oct, Jan, Apr, Jul, Oct, Jan, <u>Apr</u>
1 Jun	Jun	Jul	Oct, Jan, Apr, Jul, Oct, Jan, Apr
1 Jul	Jul	<u>Aug</u>	Oct, Jan, Apr, Jul, Oct, Jan, Apr
1 Aug	Aug	<u>Sep</u>	Oct, Jan, Apr, Jul, Oct, Jan, Apr, <u>Jul</u>
1 Sep	Sep	Oct	Jan, Apr, Jul, Oct, Jan, Apr, Jul
1 Oct	Oct	Nov	Jan, Apr, Jul, Oct, Jan, Apr, Jul
1 Nov	Nov	<u>Dec</u>	Jan, Apr, Jul, Oct, Jan, Apr, Jul, <u>Oct</u>
1 Dec	Dec	Jan	Apr, Jul, Oct, Jan, Apr, Jul, Oct

APPENDIX VI

EXTRACT OF ENERGY FUTURES CONTRACTS

Contract	Location	Size	Price	Delivery
Brent	London	1000bbls	$/bbl	cash settlement
Gas Oil	London	100 tonnes	$/MT	fob ARA
Fuel Oil	London	100 tonnes	$/MT	cash settlement
Dubai*	London	1000 bbls	$/bbl	cash settlement
WTI	New York	1000 bbls	$/bbl	fob Cushing, Okla
Heating Oil	New York	42000 galls	c/gall	fob New York Harbor
Gasoline	New York	42000 galls	c/gall	fob New York Harbor
Fuel Oil	New York	1000 bbls	$/bbl	fob New York Harbor
Fuel Oil	Singapore	100 tonnes	$/MT	fob Singapore
Dubai*	Singapore	1000 bbls	$/bbl	cash settlement

*These two contracts use the same basis for cash settlement and expire at the same time on the same day, making them effectively the same contract although they are cleared separately.

APPENDIX VII

EXTRACT OF FINANCIAL FUTURES CONTRACTS

Directory of principal 3-month interest rate and currency futures and options contracts

Contract	Exchanges	Contract Size	Minimum Price Movement	Equating to
Interest Rates				
Euro dollar	CME/LIFFE	$1m	0.01%	$25.00
Euro Deutschmark	LIFFE	DM1m	0.01%	DM25.00
Domestic sterling	LIFFE	£0.5m	0.01%	£12.50
Domestic French franc	MATIF	FF5m	0.01%	FF125.00
Currencies				
British pound	CME	£62,500	0.01 US cents/£	$12.50
Deutschmark	CME	DM125,000	0.01 US cents/DM	$125.0
Japanese yen	CME	JY12.5m	0.01 US cents/JY	$12.50
Swiss franc	CME	SF125,000	0.01 US cents/SF	$12.50

APPENDIX VIII

A GLOSSARY OF STANDARD TERMS

Backwardation When nearby futures prices are at a premium to forward prices.
Bear An investor or speculator who expects prices to fall.
Beta A factor used to calculate the degree of correlation between the index and a particular route.
Bid A firm order to buy at a stated price. (As opposed to 'offer'.)
Biffex Baltic International Freight Futures Exchange.
Brokerage The commission charged by a broker to his clients.
Bull An investor or speculator who expects prices to rise.
Capesize A vessel whose size prohibits the transit of the Panama Canal. (Usually assumed to be 100,000 deadweight and upwards.)
Clearing house The organisation through which futures contracts are fulfilled, and the banker to the exchange.
Close The final official price of the day.
Contango When nearby futures prices are at a discount to forward prices.
Contract of Affreightment A contract between a shipowner and a charterer to carry more than one cargo on voyage basis (q.v.).
Deposit A client's initial payment to his broker to open a futures position.
Forward contract A contract to buy or sell a commodity at some time in the future.
Handysize A vessel of about 25/40,000 deadweight.
Hedging The establishment of an opposite position in the futures market from that held in the physical market, as a protection from price fluctuation.

Long A bought open position (as opposed to 'short').

Lot Minimum quantity traded on market floor.

OBO A vessel (usually capesize) capable of carrying ores, bulk cargoes or oil.

Offer A firm order to sell at a stated price. (As opposed to 'Bid'.)

Open outcry In order for floor members to hear the traded prices, bids and offers are made in the market in a voice loud enough to be heard round the trading ring.

Open position A bought or sold futures contract which has not been liquidated.

Settlement The crediting or debiting to a client's account of the profit or loss realised on the closing of a futures contract.

Short A sold open position. (As opposed to 'long'.)

Time charter The shipping equivalent of hiring a car, i.e. the chartering of a vessel to be used at the charterer's disposal within a given period of time.

Variation margin In the event of a bought contract declining in value, or a sold contract increasing in value, the broker will request a payment from the client to meet the changing value of the contract; also payment by floor member to clearing house.

Voyage charter The shipping equivalent of hiring a taxi, i.e. a contract to carry a specific cargo on specific terms from point A to point B.

INDEX

Asset-play, 10–11
Association of Futures Brokers and
 Dealers, 98
Automated trading systems, 137–140
 inevitability, 138
 role of, 138
 voice of activation technology, 139

Backwardation, meaning, 175
Baltic Freight Index (BFI), 25–35, 149–152
 accuracy of, 35
 amendment of route, 155
 bull run, 30
 buying or selling for set forward date,
  36–37
 calculation of index expectations, 152
 cash settlement, and, 26–27
 charterer's decision-making process,
  39
 comment on, 32
 Committee, 149
 comparative chart of prices, 46
 constituent routes, 153–157
 construction of, 27–30
 contract specification, 78
 criticisms of, 32
 daily compilation, 29
 daily route indices, 150–151
 hedging on, 36–64. *See also* Hedging
  on BIFFEX
 how computed, 149–150
 important routes, 28
 "inception day", 149–150
 indicator, as, 34
 individual route indices, 151
 introduction of new routes, 155
 introduction of time charter routes,
  155
 London brokers, and, 34
 macro-economic factors affecting, 31
 minor amendments to route
  definitions, 155
 movement, 30–35
 New York brokers, and, 34

Baltic Freight Index (BFI)—*cont.*
 overall picture, 33
 panel, 29
 "parallelism", 30
 record low, 30
 seasonality, 30
 sensitivity of, 35
 shipping futures, 78
 significant levels, 31
 since 4.1.85, 159–168
 stock market, and, 34
 time charter element, 29
 usefulness as indicator, 31
 volatility of market, and, 34
 voyage rates, 28
 weighting factors for component
  routes, 150, 151
Baltic Freight Index 1985/90, 3
 year-on-year comparison, 32
Baltic Freight Index 1988/90—linear, 29
Baltic Futures Exchange
 amalgamation of markets, 131
 changes in, 130–131
Baltic Tanker Index. *See* TIFFEX
Bank of England US Dollar trade-weighted
 index, 90
Basis, meaning 81–82
Bear, meaning, 175
Beta, meaning, 175
Bid, meaning, 175
BIFFEX
 meaning, 175
 table of contract availability, 169
 volume traded on, 142
Brent Index, 26
Broker, 99–109
 account opening deposit, 105
 agreement on terms, 104
 authorised, 99
 cash-flow, 118
 choice in UK, 100–101
 "churning", 103
 clearer, 100
 "clipping", 103

177

Broker—*cont.*
  commission rates, 101–104
  completed trading form, 107
  continuing relationship, 108–109
  "crossing", 103
  deposit levels, 104
  finance, 118
  financial standing, 101
  "front running", 103
  independent, 100
  initial deposit, 117
  initial margin, 117
  integrity, 101
  interest, 118
  "locals", 100
  maintenance margin, 117
  "non-segregated" account, 105–106
  opening account papers, 104–105
  probity, 101
  proven track record, 101–102
  proven trading record, 102–109
  relationship with, 99–109
  relationship with client, 115–118
  reputation, 101
  "segregated" account, 105
  trading, 106–107
  types of, 99–100
  variation margin, 117
Brokerage, meaning, 175
Bull, meaning, 175
Bunker price risk, management and control, 13

Capesize, meaning, 175
Capital investment, 11–12
Cash settlement, 25–27
  Baltic Freight Index, and, 26–27
  delivery of cash, 26
  inconvenience of procedures, and, 26
  move towards, 26
Chicago Mercantile Exchange, 25
Clearing house, meaning, 175
Clearing house system, 113–115
Close, meaning, 175
Commodities exchanges, amalgamation of, 136
Commodities markets, move to futures markets, 134–135
Contango, meaning, 175
Contract of affreightment, meaning, 175
Contract month, 45, 47
Currency futures, 91
Currency risk, 14

Demand
  grain, 4–5
  steel industry, 4
Deposit, meaning, 175
Derivatives markets, future expansion, 132
Dry Cargo Freight Futures, 25–35

Dry cargo freight futures hedge, calculation of, 44–64
Dry cargo hedging, BIFFEX, using, 62–63
Dry cargo market slump 1986–87, 1

Energy futures, contract, 171
European Commodities Exchange, 135

Financial futures, contract, 172
Financial futures and options, 89–95
Financial hedging, 89–95
  futures, using 89–92
  graph of DM 62 call option at expiry, 93
  graph of 92.50 put option at expiry, 94
  options, using, 92–95
  right to buy, 92–93
  right to sell, 93–94
Financial risk, 14, 89
Forward contract, meaning, 175
Freight futures, reasons for lack of success, 142–143
Freight futures hedging
  availability of forward cover, 41
  basic principle, 36–38
  basis hedge, 43
  blanket hedge, 43
  comparative chart of BIFFEX prices, 46
  decisions to be made by potential hedger, 41
  developments of simple stratagem, 42–44
  expansion hedge, 42–43
  positioning hedge, 42
  refinements of simple stratagem, 42–43
  risk exposure, and, 38–41
  shipowner's decision-making process, 40
  simple stratagem, 38–43
Freight market, turn, 5
Freight market risk, management and control, 13
Further reading, 147
Futures broker. *See also* Broker
  view of market, 6
Futures contract
  particular, 134
  specialised, 134
Future developments, 129–140
Futures hedging, 16–23
  "dynamic hedgers", 22
  flexibility, 18
  forward contract, and, 17
  functioning of market, 21
  individual requirements of traders, 19
  insurance aspect, 22
  loss, and, 23

INDEX

Futures hedging—*cont.*
  price-fixing aspect, 22
  principle, 16–18
  psychology of, 21–23
  regulated futures exchange, 19–20
  risk management, and, 17
  scientific calculation of basis risk, 21
  speculation, and, 22
  trade allocated to particular sale, 23
  working of, 18–21
Futures prices, 109–111
  clearing house system, 113–115
  Gulf/Japan equivalents, 57
  International Stock Exchange Mnemonics, 110
  monitoring, 111
  trading disciplines, 111–112
  typical BIFFEX screen, 110
  volatility, 109–110
Futures trading
  broker-client relationship, 115–118. *See also* Broker
  cost, 113–118
  Financial Services Act, 98
  practicalities, 97–118
  regulatory regimes, 97–98
  relationship with futures broker, 99–109. *See also* Broker
  self-regulation, 98

Gas Oil contract, 20–21
  quantity unit, 20
  scope, 20
  specification, 20–21
Globex, 137
Glossary, 175

Handysize, meaning, 175
Hedging, 13–23
  meaning, 175
Hedging on BIFFEX, 36–64. *See also* Baltic Freight Index; Freight futures hedging
  BFI, correlation with, 48–52
  "broad-brush" correlation, 52
  calculating level of hedge, 52–57
    time charters, 58–63. *See also* Time charters
  calculating size of hedge, voyage charters, 57–58
  calculation of dry cargo freight futures hedge, 44–63
  catastrophe insurance, 52
  contract, 44–48
    month, 45–47
    terms, 47–48
    value, 47
  "correlation coefficient", 51
  detail, 44–64
  dry cargo, 63–64
  example of reasonable correlation, 49, 50

Hedging on BIFFEX—*cont.*
  BFI vs trade route, 49, 50
  "freight futures ready-reckoner", 55
  futures prices, 53
  relating futures prices to reality, 54
    direct proportion method, 54
    historic rate method, 54–55
    quick estimate method, 55–57
  "visual correlation analysis", 51–52
  voyage hedge calculation worksheet, 58
  ways of assessing correlations, 48

Interest rate futures, 89–91
Interest rate risk, 14
International Petroleum Exchange, 26, 80
Investment policy, need for, 8

LIFFE, expansion of, 129
London Derivatives Exchange, 129, 135
London International Financial Futures Exchange 25
London Metals Exchange, 130
London Tanker Brokers Panel, 76
London Terminal Markets, 130
London Traded Options Market, 129
Long, meaning, 176
Lot, meaning, 176

New York Mercantile Exchange, 80

OBO, meaning, 176
Offer, meaning, 176
Oil futures, 71–88
  basis trading, 81–83
    separation of supply and pricing of physical oil, 82
  "blanket hedge", and, 79
  bunker fuel price, 79–80
  exchange for physicals, 84–86
    differential, agreement as to, 85
    example, 85
    separation of price and supply, 86
  "fail-safe" clause, 83
  fixed price purchases and sales, 87
  fuel oil contract, 80
  IPE contracts, 80
  over-the-counter markets, 86–88
    counterparty, transaction with, 86–87
    expense of, 88
    swaps, 87
    trigger pricing, 87
  physical transaction, 84–86
  sale on buyer's call, 83–84
  sale on buyer's call/trigger pricing, 83–84
  shipowner, for, 79–88
  straightforward hedge, 81
  trigger pricing, 83–84

180 INDEX

Oil futures—*cont.*
    Wall Street refiners, 86
Oil output, tanker demand, and, 71
Open outcry, meaning, 176
Open position, meaning, 176

Pacific basin, 2
Physical hedging, 14–16
    disadvantages, 15
    meaning, 14
    over-the-counter options, 15
    swaps, 15
Revenue flows, 11
Risk
    definition, 8–9
    desirability, 9
    nature of shipping industry, and, 7
    necessity for, 9
    size of, 9
    unwanted, means to remove, 11–12
Risk management, skilful use of, 141
Risk pendulum, stopping, 1–11
Risk/reward parabola, 10
Risk transference media, 119

Settlement, meaning, 176
Shipowner
    oil futures for. *See* Oil futures
    use of financial futures and options.
        See Financial futures and options
Shipping, future for, 1–11
Shipping market, cycles, 5–6
Short, meaning, 176
Singapore International Monetary
    Exchange, 80
SOFFEX, 137–138
Speculation, 119–127
    aim of, 120–122
    analysis of price action, 123
    chart patterns, 123
    fundamental analysis of market, 121–127
        demand, 121
        supply less demand, 121–127
    "futures funds", 126
    "guaranteed fund", 126
    "Individual Managed Portfolio", 125–126
    liquidity of market, and, 119–120
    making trading decisions, 124
    margining system, 125
    methods, 120–127
    practices, 120–127
    "spreads", 126
    "stop loss" trading, 124–125
    technical analysis, 122–124

Speculation—*cont.*
    trading disciplines, 124
Steel industry, 4
Stock market, 34
Supply/demand equation, analysis of, 4

Tanker demand, 74
    oil output, and, 73
Tanker fleet, age profile, 2
Tanker freight futures, 65–78
    balance of tanker supply and demand, 74
    freight risk, 71
    market fluctuations, 66
    "open" contracts, and, 76–77
    "priming the pump", 65–66
    tanker demand, 74
    tanker freight rates, 75–77
    tanker supply, 72–73
    "TIFFEX", 66
    VLCC AG/West, 76
    volatility of market, 69
    world seaborne oil trade, 74
    "yardstick", 76
    1986 experiment 65–70. *See also*
        TIFFEX
        reasons for failure, 69–70
    1990 Contract, 71–78
Tanker spot rate trends, 72
Thatcherite expansion, 129–132
TIFFEX, 66
    composition of, 67
    details of contract, 67
    difficulty with contract, 67–69
Time charter hedge calculation worksheet, 61–62
Time charters, 58–63
    calculating level of hedge, 58–63
        "blanket hedge", 62
        rule of thumb method, 59–60, 60–61
        worksheet, 61–62
        voyage estimate method, 58
    detailed analysis of rates, 60
    meaning, 176
Trading, machinery of, 106–109
Trading disciplines, 111–112
Tonnage, over-supply, 8

Variation margin, meaning, 176
Voyage charter, meaning, 176
Voyage hedge calculation worksheet, 58
Voyage rates, 28

Wall Street refiners, 86